Praise for
LeaderShock . . . And How to Triumph over It

"The eight LeaderShock rules come together to form a powerful roadmap for a fresh brand of leadership right when we need it the most. Hundreds of leaders within our company—from senior managers to first-time supervisors—have become thriving leaders by following these simple steps. Without question, *LeaderShock*—the book—should be required reading for every leader in the 21st century. And LeaderShock—the term—will undoubtedly become part of everyone's business vocabulary."

> *Dean O'Hare*
> *Chairman and CEO, The Chubb Corporation*

"Greg's book gives us what we've all been waiting for—a powerful and timely new way to lead. Embrace these eight rules—you will feel masterful and invigorated. A must read for anyone working to build a healthy, thriving workplace or community."

> *Martha D. Newman*
> *Executive Director, Health Forum*

"Greg Hicks has named the epidemic all leaders must fight—LeaderShock. Fortunately, he's also developed the ultimate cure and shares it clearly and concisely. The best leadership book I've read, its eight precepts truly cross cultural and geographical boundaries with extraordinary effect."

> *Gary Owcar*
> *President, CNA Global*

"The LeaderShock model presents a practical guide for leaders at all levels in our complex, high-stress world. Over and over, I've watched it transform overwhelmed and reactive managers into highly effective and energized leaders. With this important book, Greg Hicks now gives everyone that same essential opportunity."

> *David Kelso*
> *Executive V.P. of Finance and Strategy, Aetna, Inc.*

"LeaderShock is a brilliant concept and a brilliant book. Greg Hicks cuts right to the core of what gives today's leaders a clear-cut advantage—both personally and professionally. To experience the exhilaration and effectiveness you want, adopt the eight rules as your minute-by-minute approach to leadership."

> *Dr. Joseph Mori*
> *Chairman, Dept. of Business and Finance, San Jose State Univ.*

"During the last 25 years I've been exposed to dozens of leadership programs, books and speakers. None have come close to the lasting and profound effects of Greg Hicks' eight LeaderShock rules. After embracing these principles, our leaders began to operate in a whole new way—me included. As a result we finally feel 'on-top' of our business issues. We're less stressed and more cohesive. This book will forever change the way you lead."

> *David Fowler*
> *CEO, TCI*

LEADERSHOCK
—AND HOW TO TRIUMPH OVER IT

Eight Revolutionary Rules for Becoming a Powerful and Exhilarated Leader

GREG HICKS

McGraw-Hill

New York   Chicago   San Francisco
Lisbon   London   Madrid   Mexico City   Milan
New Delhi   San Juan   Seoul   Singapore
Sydney   Toronto

1 2 3 4 5 6 7 8 9 0   DOC/DOC   0 9 8 7 6 5 4

ISBN 0-07-143916-1

Hardcover edition ISBN 0-07-140801-0 © 2003.

LeaderShock® is a registered trademark of Foster, Hicks and Associates. All other trademarked products mentioned are used in an editorial fashion only, and to the benefit of the trademark owner, with no intention of infringement of the trademark. Where such designations appear in this book, they have been printed with initial caps.

McGraw-Hill books are available at special quantity discounts to use as premiums and sales promotions, or for use in corporate training programs. For more information, please write to the Director of Special Sales, Professional Publishing, McGraw-Hill, Two Penn Plaza, New York, NY 10121-2298. Or contact your local bookstore.

 This book is printed on recycled, acid-free paper containing a minimum of 50% recycled de-inked fiber.

To my parents,
Lenore and Don Hicks

CONTENTS

ACKNOWLEDGMENTS

First, I thank the thirty-plus companies who over the last five years entrusted me to enter their realms, look at their underbellies and study LeaderShock in all its incarnations. I'm also indebted to the hundreds of thriving leaders around the globe who shared their experiences, struggles and triumphs. Their generosity and dedication to a fresh brand of leadership is embodied in these pages. I especially want to mention those who went the extra mile: Dino Robusto for his incisive intellect; Barrie Hathaway for his enormous heart; Tim Mitchell for his sparkling wisdom; David Fowler for his unwavering support; and Diane Jarmolow for giving me the best example of how high-intentioned leaders create astonishing results. It is these people who offer all of us hope for a business world built on truth and accountability.

Beyond my research compatriots, I'm grateful to many others:

To Dick Ridington, my dedicated editor who pushed me to write the concise book I always intended. More than once I pleaded, "No, we can't cut *that* line!" We always did and he was always right. Thanks also to Kathryn Black and Ariel Jolicoeur for their editorial wisdom.

To my bicoastal manuscript advisers—all wonderful friends and thriving leaders in their own right. In New York I had my "Breakfast Club"—Valerie Aguirre, Mike Allren, Susan Murphy, and Mary Ann Spatola. As insightful readers they graciously gave up a series of Sundays to meet for bagels, laughter, debate, and no-holds-barred feedback fests, all of which shaped this book. On the West Coast I utilized the brains and talents of Laurie Grassman, David Spear, and Ellen Tussman. A more candid and loyal group you may never be lucky enough to find.

To the vibrant and embracing city of Barcelona where much of this book was written. Thanks to the staff of Hotel Regencia Colon for nurturing me through my self-imposed writer's retreat.

To Van Vu. Everyone needs a genius in his life, and he's mine. Thank you for sharing your incredible gifts.

To Will and Alish Schutz who have taught me so much about human behavior and the concept of choice.

To Angela Miller, my agent, who hung in there through each phase of the proposal process and found me my new home at McGraw-Hill. It was there I had the great fortune to collaborate with Mary Glenn, Executive Editor, my trusted advocate who listened, granted my wishes, and beautifully finalized this book. Mary, you made it exciting.

A hearty thanks also to Ruth Mannino and her team at McGraw-Hill.

To my children, Tim and Molly. Thanks for unconditionally supporting my crazy schedule, challenging me to be the best person I can be, and filling me up with so much joy. I love you both.

Finally, I believe for each of us there's someone who's perfectly designed to push us to achieve far more than we ever thought possible. Rick Foster is that person for me. As cocreator of the original happiness model and my fellow glutton for the banquet of life, I'm extremely grateful for his unending ideas, expert editing and unselfish encouragement. Rick, without you the LeaderShock odyssey wouldn't have been as profound or nearly as much fun.

LEADERSHOCK
—AND HOW TO TRIUMPH OVER IT

LEADERSHOCK

THE MANAGEMENT CRISIS
OF OUR TIME

From the Oval Office in Washington, D.C. to a home office in Vancouver, B.C., the landscape of leadership has dramatically shifted over the past decade. Leaders at all organizational levels and all over the world now share something in common. They're

- *Overwhelmed* by the complexity of responsibilities and continual shifts in the marketplace

- *Overloaded* by too much to do, too much information to process, and too many demands by senior management, investors, and customers

1

- *Overstressed* by high-maintenance employees, crisis management, and increasing fears of an uncertain future.

These are the hallmarks of what I've come to call LeaderShock, and they resonate with almost every manager I talk to these days. The LeaderShock symptoms I've described cause leaders to feel frustrated, fearful, and sometimes ineffective in the one role that consumes more time than any other. Step back and think—how crazy is it *not* to demand that this huge part of your life leave you feeling masterful and invigorated?

There's good news ahead.

Consulting with Fortune 500 companies, small businesses, nonprofits, and government agencies, I've transformed thousands of victims of LeaderShock into powerful and exhilarated leaders, people who have taken back their personal sense of capability, and done so in a humane way that neither overpowers nor demeans others. Through years of research I developed both a revolutionary way to lead and a unique cure for this LeaderShock epidemic. Not only has my program worked for thousands of leaders in my clients' companies, it's changed my life, too. This book presents the essence of my revolutionary LeaderShock Program.

What makes the program unique? Long ago I came to the realization that despite what many business books and gurus say, there is no universally applicable model of leadership qualities, traits, approaches, activities, or competencies. Such prescriptions can't work because great leadership depends on calling upon your own strengths and personality to adapt to each situation.

To that end, this book offers a radically different solution: a practical roadmap of eight leadership behaviors you can use regardless of your personality, experience level, organizational culture, title, gender, ethnicity, or the economic climate in which you work. What makes these behaviors so universal and so effective is that they disarm the eight traps lurking in today's business culture and reveal the previously hidden route to getting both the business results you need *and* the personal fulfillment you want. More than mere painkillers, the eight behaviors cure the patient of the disease I call LeaderShock.

The eight behaviors (herein translated into eight rules) form the modern elixir of leadership. Mix them together and something magical and synergistic happens: Everything falls into place. All the outside forces you can't control—the market, the labor force, your boss—no longer control you. You're sitting squarely in the driver's seat.

Even better, the eight behaviors are cognitive and conscious—you *can* learn them. I've seen these rules work with leaders from every part of the world, engaged in every field, salespeople, accountants, insurance underwriters, engineers, fundraisers, politicians, even undertakers!

MY INTENTION

My intention in writing this book is to provoke you to new action and ignite a powerful excitement about your own leadership role. My fondest wish is to see you triumph over an environment often fraught with both global and local tensions and discontent. By sharing what I know about the behaviors of exhilarated and powerful leaders, I'll show you how to

- Reverse the personal toll of leadership by allowing you to stop working long hours and absorbing undue stress so you have energized time left over for the richness of life outside of work

- Achieve the business results you want, the recognition you deserve, and the endorphin rush of pure productivity

- Lead with competence and humanity at a time when human issues loom larger than ever

The world needs trust and faith in its leaders. You are an ambassador of hope, the navigator through the inevitable challenges that lie ahead Whatever your previous path, you're now the one we look to lead with confidence and vigor in these uncertain times. Never before has your role been so critical.

MY JOURNEY TO THE LEADERSHOCK CURE

I've been on a long, often surprising, sometimes frustrating, always fascinating journey toward developing and solidifying the eight-step LeaderShock cure. For half a decade I've been fine-tuning my program through practical application in business seminars and collaboration with a host of experts in their fields, and I've had the privilege of intimately observing the unique cultures of more than thirty companies—from tiny nonprofits to colossal global corporations. Most of all, through in-depth interviews, I've had the benefit and pleasure of learning directly from well over 200 exemplary leaders from around the world who are personally and professionally thriving.

My journey began with direct experience. I worked as a leader in a multinational company for fifteen years, managing others and being managed. I had wonderful bosses and unbearable ones. And, as a boss, I suffered many LeaderShock symptoms myself. Ultimately, I felt unfulfilled and went into business for myself.

Though my new leadership consulting practice was booming, I realized early on that something was wrong. Regardless of any immediate success I experienced with teams and groups of leaders, the long-term sustainability of my work was affected by a pervasive, culturewide unhappiness. After a while I began feeling disheartened by my efforts and saturated with the workplace misery surrounding me. I wanted to explore something more positive and uplifting. Just what, I wasn't sure.

That's when my partner, Rick Foster, and I came up with the idea that forever changed our lives. Since our work took us all over the world, we decided to tack a couple of days onto each trip and search out profoundly happy people and interview them. We weren't looking for the perpetually cheery, put-on-a-happy-face variety, but those rare individuals who just seem to have life wired.

The "happiness project," as we dubbed it, rekindled our excitement. We cut back our consulting practice and, over the next three years, spent half our time visiting towns and cities across America and Europe. We'd walk into markets or coffee shops and simply ask the locals, "Who's the happiest person around?" They'd caucus, proffer a name and we'd call that person and invite ourselves over. Not once were we turned down. Two and a half years later, we had been in more than 300 living rooms engaging in intimate discussions about the fundamental nature of happiness. Regardless of their dramatically different life circumstances, these people were, amazingly enough, all making the *same* behavioral choices.

Our research culminated in the book, *How We Choose to Be Happy* (Putnam, 1999), a description of the principles by which anyone can become a happier person. Even before the book was completed, I found myself fascinated by a subset of the people we'd interviewed. They were all in leadership roles—as corporate managers, directors of nonprofits, small business owners, and community leaders—and I began to notice that they had something in common. None showed any signs of the Leader-Shock syndrome I'd watched consume the lives of my clients. As I got to know them better, I saw that they enjoyed reputations unequaled in their fields for attaining profitability and motivating people.

I wanted to know why, and devoted the next several years to playing detective. Before I was done I'd been everywhere from San Diego to Budapest, talking with and observing leaders at work who weren't merely surviving the complex demands of their positions, but thriving. I listened to their stories during interviews averaging three hours and recorded their philosophies and practices. Behind the closed doors of businesses and organizations I dissected meetings and observed leaders in their most private interactions as they strove to meet the challenges that came with their territories. There was a striking difference between those who struggled and those who thrived. And a certain mystery attended the thrivers.

- They worked fewer hours than their colleagues, yet consistently achieved better results and therefore were seen by senior management as critical to their organization's success.

- They were known as tough and direct, yet their people felt motivated, valued, and appreciated. As a result, their people went the extra mile for them.

- They were less negatively affected by global and company problems and felt invigorated in their leadership role.

Over time I saw that these thriving leaders were truly visionaries, making choices that ran almost directly counter to their organizational cultures. In fact, as I discovered, the business culture that surrounds us all is, itself, the source of LeaderShock. It has us putting out fires, being victimized by forces outside our control, taking actions that don't play to talents, burdening ourselves with too much responsibility, and committing to plans that change before they can even be implemented. In short, that culture sabotages our ability to succeed by pushing us to perpetuate the LeaderShock traps you'll read about in this book.

GETTING STARTED

The principles at the heart of this book, while tried and true, require two things from you. First, you must be willing to take a hard look in the mirror and do some honest self-analysis. Second, you must be open to embracing a new set of behaviors for the way you lead. These universal principles won't dictate what you should believe, what kind of personality you should have, or how you should say things. And they won't require any particular set of personal goals or desires other than the desire to be effective and feel fulfilled in leading others. They simply suggest that the part of your life that occupies more time than any other should leave you feeling masterful and invigorated.

People I've worked with consistently tell me they've experienced sustainable change as they integrate the eight rules. I often hear words to this effect: "Now I realize how out of control I was. Before the roadmap out of LeaderShock, the stress had taken its toll. I'm so much happier. For the first time in years I feel like I'm truly leading."

Now I invite you to join them and take the leap for yourself—out of the turmoil of LeaderShock and into true leadership!

ACTIVATE INTENTIONS

"Nothing can stop the man with the right mental attitude from achieving his goals: Nothing on earth can help the man with the wrong mental attitude."

—Thomas Jefferson

In the throes of LeaderShock, we merely react to one event after the next. With so many demands coming from so many directions, our business culture kicks in and demands rapid fire responses. It insists we *do* something, anything, to fix each problem. The result: Often, we don't get the outcomes we really want. What's missing is a preliminary step, pivotal to us yet invisible to everyone else. That pivotal step involves our Intention, the key to mobilizing the untapped force that lies within us and the axle on which the other seven rules turn.

I've taught even the most hardened Wall Street executives how to harness the power of their Intentions to get the trust, invigoration, and business results they want without domineering, creating departmental strife, or pushing their own stress levels to the stratosphere. The fact is, unlike forces we can't control, our Intentions are 100 percent *within our control*. Yet most distracted and overwhelmed leaders fail to capitalize on that reality, and instead stumble from one activity to the next on autopilot—all because they are unaware of their Intentions.

But whether we're aware of them or not, our Intentions are driving the show. Minute by minute, they are the internal messages we give ourselves that dictate not only what we say, but how we say it, how we act, and how we are perceived. When we're not conscious of our Intentions, they become like runaway stallions, taking us to places we don't want to go. (Thus that out-of-control feeling that goes with LeaderShock.) By making clear, purposeful Intentions, we focus in a chosen direction and act optimally.

Simple, yet subtle, Rule No. 1 consists of two equally important steps:

1. Consciously set your Intention before any event—prior to a customer call, at the outset of a meeting, or before interacting with employees.

2. Then fully reveal that Intention (that is, your most closely held work-related desires, motivations, and internal game plans) to whomever you're working with.

If that sounds too radical or simply undoable, allow me to guide you down the rabbit hole to the Wonderland of Intention.

STEP ONE: SETTING YOUR INTENTION

You set your Intention by seizing the invaluable yet fleeting window of opportunity that occurs between perceiving something and reacting to it. Therein is the triumphal turning point away from LeaderShock to something sublimely better. Here's how it works: Before any interaction or event take an extra few seconds to transform your outcome by consciously choosing how you want to respond. During these precious seconds you establish your Intention by predetermining the two leadership elements that affect everything—your *attitude* and *behavior*.

Attitude is always the place to begin because it colors everything you're about to do.

ATTITUDE

Determine your attitude by asking yourself these three questions:

- *What's my attitude now?* (For example: Am I apathetic? Hostile?)

- *Does this attitude get me what I really want?* (If you're apathetic or hostile, your answer is probably, "No.")

- *If not, what attitude will get me what I want?* (An invigorated attitude? A compassionate one?)

If you're struggling with these questions, I challenge you to embrace the following truth: *Regardless of your situation, you can always choose your attitude.* Perhaps you don't believe it? Well, if you have control over what you order from a restaurant menu or your position on a political issue, you have that same control over your own attitude. Your frame of mind is actually whatever you want it to be. The problem is that in the grip of LeaderShock you're so busy *doing* that you don't take time to choose your attitude, so you allow it to control you rather than the reverse.

"The greatest discovery of my generation is that a human being can alter his life by altering his attitude."

—William James

Because attitude animates your actions, once your attitude is set you're in the best position to decide what behavior is going to work best.

BEHAVIOR

Good news: Everything you just did to choose your attitude will also help you choose the behavior you want. Ask yourself the same three questions, slightly modified:

- *What behavior am I about to engage in?* (For example: Give my employee a hard time. Persuade my boss I'm right?)

- *Does this get me what I really want?*

- *If not, what behavior will work better?*

Consider some approaches: Do I want to just listen right now, offer full support, gather as much feedback as I can before making any comments, aggressively make my point, or play devil's advocate? Your list of choices is limited only by your imagination. But once you choose, you've created a behavioral strategy that optimizes the chances for a positive result.

Windows of Opportunity

With a little practice the act of choosing attitude and behavior becomes a lightning-fast process that you activate as naturally as you brush your teeth or fasten your seatbelt. *As your day unfolds, the more opportunities you seize to set your attitude and behavior, the more empowered, and the less LeaderShocked, you'll be.* Thriving leaders have not fallen into the Crisis Reactor Trap and you don't need to either. With a determination to find these opportunities to set your Intention, you stop merely reacting and become the master of who you want to be and how you want to be seen by others.

My experience with thousands of leaders has convinced me that what you achieve, your end result, is based almost entirely on the nature and strength of your Intentions, and very little on the actual things you do to get there. That's why creating deliberate Intentions is the ultimate transformational leadership behavior, even under dire circumstances.

> *"We who lived in concentration camps can remember the men who walked through the huts comforting others, giving away their last piece of bread. They may have been few in number, but they offer sufficient proof that everything can be taken away from a man but one thing: the last of the human freedoms—to choose one's attitude in any given set of circumstances, to choose one's own way."*
>
> —Victor Frankl,
> *Man's Search for Meaning*

Though few leaders find themselves in the unthinkable scenario described by Victor Frankl, I've watched managers with ill-conceived Intentions languish and managers with well-considered Intentions transcend the LeaderShocked masses to become stars. To prove that point, let's explore two leaders from two companies: Michael, an upbeat, gregarious, seat-of-the-pants powerhouse, and Mary Ann, a soft-spoken, highly organized engineer. On the surface they appear to be as different as night and day, yet each has not only avoided Leader-Shock but thrived in the chaos of modern business. Both are effective leaders, both are invigorated leaders, and both use Intentions in ways that suit their unique styles.

The Purposeful Powerhouse

Michael, the Denver manager of a small plastics company, supervises eight sales representatives. Last year his top-rated department grew three times faster than the sales departments in any of the other six offices. "I lead by Intention. It's everything. I set my Intentions fifty times a day, maybe more. Before I do anything, I check my control panel. I come in for a landing with all my instruments adjusted for success."

So one morning after Bob, an employee, landed a new account, Michael was ready with a well-thought out Intention rather than the standard pat on the back. He motioned Bob into his office and purposely projected the enthusiastic pride he felt (attitude) as he asked probing questions about why Bob thought he'd been so successful (behavior). The outcome was twofold: First, Bob felt charged up. Second, Bob was armed with an awareness of his success factors and the motivation to continue using them in the long term.

Michael's day went from rushed to hectic. Susan, another staff member, began leaving some not-so-subtle clues that she was annoyed. Rather than give in to the urge to ignore her, he set an Intention to convey empathy (attitude), and to find out what was wrong while offering his full attention (behavior). Once again Intention yielded the result Michael *really* wanted—an employee who walked away energized and focused rather than sulking the day away.

Michael is known for his proactive leadership, and he's reputed to deliver the most impressive presentation at quarterly board meetings. The Board of Directors who preside over this solemn event are a brutal bunch, infamous for terrorizing speakers with J. Edgar Hoover-style interrogation techniques. Where does Michael find his confidence? He overrides initial reactions of fear and tension with a healthy determination to be articulate, upbeat, and informal. Feelings of intimidation are alleviated. His reoriented frame of mind is "I'm here because I'm the expert. Nobody else knows more about my territory than I do." And because he believes it, so does the Board. Michael knows that his mindset is more powerful than anything that actually happens at the meeting. Instead of being poised for an anxiety-based interaction, Michael sets himself up for the experience *he* desires.

Like Michael, we must see ourselves as artists, choosing among an array of colors on our internal palette. We create an exquisite mixture of chosen attitudes and behaviors uniquely appropriate to the situation at hand. This enlightened awareness is what makes thriving leaders so rare.

Rising above the Fray

Mary Ann is a rare commodity at her company. When I was first hired to work with the leaders of Mary Ann's organization I was told to brace myself. "This group is miserable, always at each other's throats," groaned the director in charge, "except for Mary Ann. She's phenomenal; a natural-born leader." Indeed, I found her to be intelligent and articulate, but that's not what made her so special. Before each of the contentious weekly leadership meetings, she was not only predetermining how she intended to make key points, she was calmly writing them down. At the meetings, in the quietest way, she always got what she wanted. Her scripted notes detailed not only what she wanted to say, but also how she intended to say it.

As a guest at several of these meetings, I witnessed a rollercoaster ride of hostile reactions and hurt feelings. Mary Ann, by contrast, never took the ride. "With this group I've got two Intentions in play at all times." she says. "Number one: I choose to not be offended regardless of what someone says to me." (Attitude) "And number two: I always listen first with the aim to understand." (Behavior) "I go in to each meeting intending to walk out with dignity and grace—and I do."

When we don't *assertively* set our Intentions, we passively or unconsciously choose something else. Our outcomes are haphazard, and we become hostage to people and events that lead us astray. It's like untying a motorboat from the dock, but neglecting to turn on the engine. We're merely adrift, buffeted by winds, currents, and the wakes of other boats—factors beyond our control. Great things may await on the other side of the lake but unless serendipity is on our side we'll never get there. Setting an Intention turns on the engine that propels us on a course we have purposely chosen. *Intention adds directionality and power to human endeavor.*

"If you think you can do a thing or think you can't do a thing, you're right."

—Henry Miller

Setting Intentions has even broader, more profound applicability when you apply it beyond situational uses to your daily and yearly leadership experience. Let's look at Intention as an antidote to LeaderShock precipitators on a grander scale.

DAY-BY-DAY INTENTIONS

If we don't watch out, the pernicious force of workplace negativity engulfs us, whether it stems from a plunging market, a problematic customer, or conflict with other departments. Even worse, we give authority to our own negative voice: "I can't do it," "I don't care any more." "It's hopeless." The cumulative strength of all this negativity can be counteracted only by the even greater strength of our commitment to a positive *daily* Intention.

Thriving leaders know that the essential "to do" when they hit their desks in the morning is *not* the traditional to-do list of activities. Before anything else they choose their attitude for the day. It's as much a ritual as that first cup of coffee. Both guarantee a terrific rush,—the former from jumping into a positive frame of mind; the later from a blast of caffeine.

Daily Intentions preset the way thriving leaders meet the events of the day. Their commitment is about creating a day that's optimistic and focused rather than scattered and stressed. As one leader put it, "I start off *expecting* to have a rich and upbeat experience every day, full of stimulating interactions, challenging puzzles, and new learning. And those expectations pay off. What I expect to get is exactly what I do get. And what I get is "The Gold.""

And so it could go for you.

"If you expect nothing, you're apt to be surprised. You'll get nothing."

—Malcolm Forbes

Choosing your day isn't about denying problems, sugarcoating them, or guaranteeing specific results. It's about intensifying your focus on that which is uplifting and self affirming. When you choose a positive attitude you feel physically better. My friend, biochemist Dr. David Spear, helped me understand why. He tells me a physiological phenomenon takes place when you give yourself any positive message (such as enjoyment, pride, or confidence). Endorphins are released, you feel better, and then more endorphins are released. It's a cycle; conscious behavior elicits biochemical reward, which in turn encourages you to generate more positive messages. Since you have the power to initiate this cycle, let me invite you to take the opportunity to do so every chance you get!

> *"Attitude, to me, is more important than facts. It's more important than the past, than education, than money, than circumstances, than failures, than successes, than what other people think or say or do. It is more important than appearance, giftedness, or skill. It will make or break a company . . . a church . . . a home. The remarkable thing is we have a choice everyday regarding the attitude will we embrace for that day. "*
>
> —Charles Swindoll

YEAR-BY-YEAR INTENTIONS

Moving beyond daily Intentions, powerful and exhilarated leaders also devise ongoing Intentions they live by all the time. These are not bench-marked goals attainable in a finite period of time (for example, "By year's end I will close five more million-dollar deals.") These are broader, grander, year-to-year commitments to ongoing attitudes and behaviors. As individual as thumbprints, you create them after assessing what attitudes and behaviors will give you the greatest payoff over time. In essence, they become your modus operandi. Here are some examples:

- I always help, never hurt.

- I make things better, never blame or become a victim.

- I spend time with the people who can get me the most return.

- I generate and embrace new ideas, not shoot them down.

- I sell and champion my team's mission every chance I get.

The magic in all these statements is that they're panoramic in application, yet narrow in focus. And that's the source of their power. *The narrower your focus, the stronger the Intention, and the stronger the Intention, the greater the likelihood you'll get what you want.* Let's take a familiar example. You've probably had the experience of hearing about a new car you've never noticed before but are now interested in. With a laser-like Intention to find one, miraculously, you begin to see that new car at every corner. And this is the point. *When you are crystal clear about what you are looking for, you begin to find it everywhere.* So it follows that when you're crystal clear about how you want to be, that's what you become.

> *"A man is but the product of his thoughts. What he thinks, he becomes."*
>
> —Mahatma Gandhi

PART TWO: STATING YOUR INTENTION

Setting Intention is only the first half of the story. One of my most important discoveries about non-LeaderShocked managers—the crème de la crème—is that they consistently make the right things happen by *stating* their Intentions. In so doing, they remove unproductive assumptions and masterfully establish just the right tenor for every process and dialogue. Most of all, by daring to disclose their Intentions they invoke the two leadership essentials—the creation of trust and mutual respect.

I believe that parlaying our internal intentions into spoken Intentions renders a breakthrough, a brand of crystal-clear communication that not only frees us all from the clutches of LeaderShock but also ushers in an exciting new wave of leadership.

Unfortunately, divulging *real* Intentions is so counter-cultural to organizational thinking that it rarely dawns on anyone to do it. In most companies leaders are taught, coached, and encouraged to protect themselves by strategically withholding their motivations, desires, and underlying reasons for personal behavior. But sadly, this lack of crucial information is the keep-your-cards-close-to-the-vest genesis of stress, frustration, and confusion—an expressway to LeaderShock.

"All serious daring starts from within."

—Eudora Welty

HOW TO STATE AN INTENTION

Stating Intentions requires that you have the courage to reveal *your internal game plan*. Whether you're addressing one of your staff members or a large audience for the first time, stand up, take a deep breath, and let everyone know right from the start

- Who you are

- What you're up to

- Where you're coming from

For maximum success, challenge yourself to state your Intentions right up front every time—at the new hire orientation meeting, during an employee coaching session to address a hygiene issue, while interacting with your boss over a missed deadline, or even at a meeting with your most irrational client. Consider Margaret's story and the impact of her spoken Intention.

KEEP THE MAIN THING THE MAIN THING

Several years ago I was working with the leaders of a large hospital. On the day our training was to begin, I watched the seventy participants shuffle into the conference room with that irritated "Why am I here?" look. No doubt about it, these people were overwhelmed by weighty workloads and didn't want to waste a whole day in a seminar. Soon a 5-foot dynamo entered the room to kick off the program. Unaware of her spellbinding powers, I fully expected to hear the usual platitudes—something about the company's commitment to developing people and hopes that everyone would take full advantage of the chance to learn. But instead, I was about to hear words I remember to this day.

Margaret, Director of the hospital, stepped to the podium. "Good morning." she said. "As head of this organization, I want to take this opportunity to restate my overriding Intention. And that is: I fully intend to turn our reputation around. I'm committed to finding every opportunity to transform us from the hospital with the lowest patient satisfaction rating in the city to the hospital with the highest. That must be your Intention as well. Everything we do from here on out is in service of raising patient satisfaction. And we must never lose focus. Today's training is imperative to removing the traps that prevent us from leading with the gusto we need to realize our Intention."

Margaret concluded with one of the most memorable Intention lines I've ever heard. *"The main thing"* she said, *"is just to keep the main thing the main thing.* And, doing everything we can to become a hospital with exemplary customer service is, unquestionably, the *main thing!"*

With those words Margaret palpably transformed the mood in that room. Now leaders of diverse viewpoints were willing to coalesce around the personal commitment of a strong and self-assured leader. Margaret not only created context for the entire day and avoided backlash, she rallied the troops around *her* vision and direction.

As Margaret demonstrated, there's no substitute for a spoken Intention. Much more than articulating an issue, it is a vigorous and relentless expression of her pledge to personal behavior. Often born from stubbornness and sheer tenacity, spoken

Intentions energize and animate employees and enrich all their subsequent actions.

"My strength lies solely in my tenacity."

—Louis Pasteur

APPLICATIONS: WITH EMPLOYEES, COWORKERS, AND TEAMS

When you start conversations with an Intention statement you've gone far beyond stating your expectations of what you want other people to do, you've revealed *how you intend to be.* Consider these examples:

- *To your employee*: "I want to give you an opportunity to take the ball and run with it on this project. I'll stay in the background until you come to me." *(With this statement, there's no question in the employee's mind as to your respective roles in this project.)*

- *To your valued colleague (after a misunderstanding)*: "My Intention is to rebuild trust between us. In the past we had a wonderful relationship that I valued very much. Somehow we got off track and I want to do my

31

part to bring us back together again." *(With any misunderstanding, an Intention statement gives you the opening you need to clean things up. Notice that three sentences, nothing fancy and a mere 15 seconds of dialogue, are the inaugural step to an honest dialogue critical to mending a broken relationship.)*

- *To your most difficult coworker (after a conflict):* "My intention is to engage with you rather than pull away. I'd like to review what happened, hear your perspective, and be able to share mine. I want to be clear with you about why I was so angry and then begin to look at ways we can work together better in the future." *(With troubled relationships, a healthy Intention statement gives both parties a constructive vehicle for collaboration, rather than being stuck in anger.)*

- *To your team:* "My Intention at this meeting is to give you the opportunity to air your concerns about this project. I want it all out on the table so that we can address things up front rather than allow issues to escalate." *(Notice how a crisp, to-the-point Intention statement turns a potentially belabored, disconnected meeting into one that's focused, time-sensitive, and comprehensive.)*

The result? Like an experienced bandleader, in each of these interactions you've set the tone and direction. Not only have you established a set of ground rules, you've constructed the stage on which anyone can join you in success. In all four examples, you've taken powerful and humane stances as a leader.

Remember, leaders are magnets for speculation at the water cooler. If you don't tell people where *you're* coming from, they'll spend hours guessing—alone, in pairs, in clusters. And those guesses will be based on whatever tidbits of data they can collect, your body language, their observations of your whereabouts, comments overheard in the hall—all signals easily misinterpreted. Once people are free from deciphering your motives, their morale and productivity have the chance to soar.

TAMING GOLIATH

Imagine an entire company where all the employees start key conversations by revealing how they intend to behave and what they desire. Beyond all else, it's one of the most efficient and upbeat business settings you'll ever experience. One of my clients, a wholly owned subsidiary of a large company in which Intention statements have become the norm, put the power of Intentions to the supreme test.

Thomas, the CEO of the subsidiary, is charismatic and intelligent and has keen insight on what makes people tick. But he was faced with one of the most challenging conversations of his career. He concluded that the subsidiary might not survive the economic downturn without acquiring a smaller company with a presence in Europe. Doing so, however, would require a large infusion of capital from the parent company.

Thomas made an appointment to meet with Mr. G., the parent's Chairman. In the past such meetings had been frustrating, even somewhat demeaning: His ideas had drawn comments like, "This is too pie-in-the-sky." or "You're doing just fine with what you've got now." Thomas typically left those meetings feeling overpowered, incompetent, and dismissed.

Needless to say, he needed this meeting to be different. He pulled together his executive leadership team to help him carve out a well-crafted Intention statement. Because the meeting with Mr. G. was so critical to the company's future, they wrote out the statement and Thomas memorized it, word for word.

When the day arrived, Thomas nervously went to the Chairman's office. First, he set his attitude at the door: confidence, focus, conviction. After a brief greeting he said, "I'd like to capture your full attention by requesting thirty minutes of your uninterrupted time. My Intention in coming here today is to be more assertive in expressing my needs to you. My aim is to get you to be my advocate, rather than my devil's advocate. I'm going to make a bold request and I'm very serious about wanting your support." Mr. G. sat upright in his chair. The ensuing discussion was difficult but the most candid the two men ever had. Mr. G. asked his secretary to hold all calls, and didn't try to minimize Thomas's request.

That night at home, Thomas replayed their discussion. It had gone well with the exception of one disturbing reaction he hadn't foreseen. Perhaps his Intention statement had been *too* strong. Mr. G. appeared to have been knocked off balance—he even looked like he felt betrayed. Once again Intention became Thomas's guidepost to refocusing Mr. G. and confronting what might be a negative situation. The next morning Thomas arrived at the home office early to see Mr. G. and clarify how he'd expressed his Intention.

"I want to clean up some loose ends." said Thomas. "I walked away yesterday sensing that you were upset." Mr. G. confirmed that he'd felt cornered. "Let me review what I meant." Thomas said. "At the heart of all my motivations right now is the desire to get the best value for my business, my employees, and ultimately you. That's what drove every one of my words yesterday."

That morning something shifted in their 20-year relationship, a mutual self-interest evolved between the two men that led to newfound respect and rapport. For the next 6 months Thomas visited Mr. G.'s office frequently and invariably began with his most honest Intentions. Even though the acquisition never took place, through candid and balanced dialogue something even more favorable did, a commitment from the Chairman to fund two new expansion projects.

As Thomas's experience shows, perseverance in communicating Intentions is often the key to gradually improving relationships and getting what you want, even when what you want seems like a long-shot. If at first things don't go well, keep going. Obviously every boss is different and no one Intention serves every situation but I have seen over and over again that when you begin conversations with an Intention statement, you level the playing field—even with someone many rungs up the ladder from you.

BREAKING THROUGH THE HIERARCHY

To show you what I mean, I'd like to introduce you to a first-year supervisor, Troy, who scheduled a meeting with Donna, the Director of Human Resources of the multinational corporation they worked for. He approached the meeting having set his attitude (self-assurance and respect for Donna) and having armed himself with a strong statement of his Intention to develop and run a support group for new supervisors. He walked out 10 minutes later with a seemingly impossible result. In the midst of a freeze on spending, Donna agreed to fund the support group. She caught up with me later and laughed, saying, "What did you teach him? He was so sincere and committed. I was putty in his hands!"

Donna's observation brings me to a warning: Insincere Intention statements backfire. Most people can sense manipulation a mile away. When you abuse the power of Intention, trust is destroyed and credibility lost. Intentions are like diamonds: To be worth anything they must be genuine.

WHAT'S IN IT FOR YOU?

Let's review some of the business benefits of expressing Intentions up front:

- Clarity and unity among employees, which leads to better results

- Open and honest dialogue with clients, coworkers, and employees that builds stronger relationships

- A healthy forum for dealing head on with conflict, fear, or volatile conversations

- An increase in employee satisfaction levels because those employees aren't frustrated and lost

- An opportunity to access your power when others attempt to control or intimidate you

There are hidden benefits as well. The first is a phenomenon I call emotional loyalty, which is an internal commitment that people make to you. When you honestly reveal your Intentions you send the message, "I trust you enough to reveal myself to you." That opens the door for them to trust you in return. You get more than their technical competence and emotional intelligence: You get the priceless gift of loyalty from people who want to rally around to support (rather than sabotage) you.

Another benefit, and perhaps the most important when it comes to freeing yourself from LeaderShock, is that setting and stating your Intentions increases your own level of satisfaction. I've devoted much of the last decade to studying the lives of profoundly happy people. One of their hallmarks is that they are purposeful in choosing their attitude and behavior. They're in control of their own lives because they continually *create* the situations they want. I can guarantee you, laying out all your Intentions, not holding them in, not disguising or adorning them, ultimately feels great!

But there is a danger in this. You've heard the expression, "The road to hell is paved with good Intentions." That might be true unless you're prepared to deliver. Intention is just the beginning. Once you declare your Intentions you *must* hold yourself accountable to take action. Go to the next step: It's time to *own it all*!

SUMMARY OF RULE ONE

LeaderShock Trap No. 1:
The Crisis Reactor

When we're bombarded with things coming at us all at once, we operate on automatic pilot, merely responding without being aware of how we want to be or proactively deciding what will ultimately work best.

New Intentions

- I set my Intention before each event of the day. I take a moment to determine the attitude and behavior that will get me what I want and have the desired impact on others.

- I state those Intentions to anyone who needs to know. I reveal my motives, thoughts, and desires at the beginning of any conversation, meeting, presentation, or event!

2

OWN IT ALL!

"In the long run we shape our lives and shape ourselves. The process never dies. And the choices we make are ultimately our own responsibility."

—Eleanor Roosevelt

Anyone in a leadership role is subject to the whims of other people and the capriciousness of unforeseen events. The competition sneaks up from behind to steal our best accounts and most valued people. New technologies bury us in unwanted information. And unlike years past, a collapse in Tokyo's money markets can now trigger layoffs for a small manufacturer in Cedar Rapids. With each year that goes by, I've watched the spiraling complexity of the business environment take its toll on managers, pushing them ever further into the maelstrom of LeaderShock.

There's something else I've noticed, however, that isn't complex at all. In fact, it's strikingly simple: The leaders most gripped by LeaderShock *see* themselves as victims of circumstance. By contrast, leaders who are undeniably thriving reject the victim role entirely, maintaining a mindset of total ownership. They shout out a philosophy that says: "I am 100 percent responsible to myself, to my Intentions, to my results, to my people, and to the kind of workforce I want to create, no matter what's going on within my division, my company, the country, or the world. I Own It All!"

But here's a jarring and sobering thought: This notion of complete ownership runs counter to most organizations' cultures and is, therefore, counterintuitive for many leaders. These are organizations that talk about accountability all the time; yet few have created anything remotely resembling an accountability culture. How do I know? Because there's a disease endemic to most companies today. It's called *blame*, and it's the greatest single symptom of nonaccountability.

For the last several years I've used an unconventional barometer to assess company climates. It involves doing a little eavesdropping as I walk through the lunchroom. Time and again the results are the same. Ninety percent of what I overhear is some version of blame. "Can you believe how hurtful she was to me?" "He made me look bad by dropping the ball on this project." And the most pervasive of all, "Now look what they're making me do!" These are examples of the "Victim" trap of LeaderShock. Sadly, this victim mentality is allowed to infect every cell of the corporate body, whether those corporate cultures consist of three coworkers or 3000.

If we are to survive, leadership must mean *emphatically refusing to blame anyone or anything for any reason.* Seem impossible?

Weeding out blame from your behavioral repertoire doesn't mean you don't hold people accountable for their actions. It *does* mean you refuse to believe that other people—your boss, your employees, your customers—are doing things *to* you. If you make the dangerous assumption that people or things control how you feel at work, you become like a king who's given away his crown. You're Leader-Shocked because you are no longer in charge.

Even though blame's seductive powers of commiseration and abdication of guilt have us in their thrall, when the blame comes home to roost, as it inevitably does, the effect is always misery. And here's why. It's virtually impossible to feel invigorated, competent, or powerful and indulge in blaming at the same time. Blame is a swamp. As soon as you stumble into it, you lose your footing and forward direction. You're immobilized, mired in the muck of your resentment and frustration. And an entire support system is stalled as its quicksand pulls down everyone around you.

"People are always blaming their circumstances for what they are. I don't believe in circumstances. The people who get on in this world are the people who get up and look for the circumstances they want, and, if they can't find them, make them."

—George Bernard Shaw

Leaders who thrive don't get bogged down. Their approach to problems looks like this: "I didn't want this to happen, but it did, so what can *I* do to make things better for myself and my team?" This becomes their Intention. Rather than feeling resentful, they aggressively choose to move to the higher ground of productivity and satisfaction. How do they get to higher ground? They go on a search.

FINDING MY PART

The thrill of leadership and the freedom from Leader-Shock, come when we look nowhere but squarely in the mirror. Whenever negative things happen to you, stop and ask the *only* question that can deliver a sense of true accomplishment and satisfaction: "What's *my* part?" As you come to better understand these three power-packed words, you find they actually break down into two supporting questions:

- *What did I do to contribute to the problem?*
  What could I have done differently? Was there a piece of this issue that belongs to me, even if it was only a small piece?

- *What can I do to make things better?*
  Can I take some action that will fix or undo the part that I played?

"What's my part?" belongs right at the forefront of your new leadership repertoire. By zeroing in on an honest assessment of your role, you avoid the worthless exercises of figuring out what other people did, wishing things were different, or wanting other people to change. In fact, consciously focusing on yourself is the *only* way to take back the crown of leadership you've unconsciously given away.

Now for some words of caution: "What's my part?" has absolutely nothing to do with blaming yourself. In fact, self-blame is the most insidious form of the blame trap. Internal dialogue such as "That was such a stupid mistake" or "Why didn't I think of that?" are self-recriminating and leave you in the same pit of resentment as any other form of blame. Rather, "What's my part?" should be seen as a vigorously analytical and self-affirming step toward growth and change.

PUTTING "MY PART" TO WORK

I interviewed a young manager, Brian, who remembered when he first learned to hold up the mirror. "I'd been assigned to a project team, and three weeks into it," he told me, "I was miserable. What a horrible experience. The boss hadn't explained our objectives. Team members weren't pulling their weight and I was getting all the work no one else wanted. On top of everything else, I felt forced to go along with the direction the team decided to take."

All Brian's perceptions were valid, but, as he realized one Friday evening, they were misdirected. "I finally got it." he told me. "The real question is not, what should *they* be doing? It's: 'What should *I* do?' So rather than having another agitated weekend, I sat down Saturday morning and made a list." See the sidebar for excerpts from Brian's list.

EXCERPTS FROM BRIAN'S LIST

- Ask for clarification from the boss.

- Give team members feedback about my concerns.

- Look more aggressively for new approaches.

- Come to the meetings with recommendations.

"When I started doing these things I immediately felt stronger, more uplifted. After I probed my boss for more clarification, I was able to give better feedback. When people on the team didn't like some of my suggestions, I thought of new ones. There wasn't nearly the frustration because I was taking full control of myself. Suddenly, what other people did or didn't do had less and less impact on me".

"Self-pity is our worst enemy and if we yield to it, we can never do anything wise in this world."

—Helen Keller

THE CASE OF THE "STICKY FINGERS"

Even when blaming seems fully justified and there's ample evidence to suggest that you're truly the wounded party, the way out of LeaderShock is still to look at your part. Valerie, the owner of a successful catering company, learned the Own It All lesson the hard way. Last year she reeled from the shock of firing her once trusted in-house accountant for embezzlement. After a painful investigation it became evident that the woman had forged checks and stolen from petty cash to the tune of $30,000.

Valerie might have chosen to see herself as the innocent victim of a crime. But she chose differently. "I knew I must have played a major role in this episode." she said. "Even though it was an unintentional role, I had to figure out how I could stop something like this from happening again."

After some soul-searching, Valerie realized she hadn't set appropriate limits for her employees and had designed bookkeeping practices without built-in controls. As a result, Valerie changed her business systems. But that was just the tip of the iceberg. More important, after finding out *what* had happened, she focused on the underlying causes of *why* it happened.

"I had desperately wanted to create a cozy family atmosphere at work. I think I actually cared more about preserving that image than about my business itself. Deep down I knew something wasn't right, but I closed my eyes to the things going on around me."

Carefully analyzing, as Valerie did, the ways in which you played a role, you begin to discover recurring behaviors that might continually undermine your success. To the extent that you see each obstacle as a chance for learning about yourself, rather than spotlighting what other people did to you, you step out from behind the walls of LeaderShock.

"Action springs not from thought, but from a readiness for responsibility."

—Dietrich Bonhoeffer

DEFENDING YOURSELF BY OWNING NOTHING

Besides blame and victimhood, there's another way we hurt ourselves. We dodge responsibility by invoking our defense mechanisms. These well-honed defenses come in a variety of forms. Here are some examples:

1. Passive defense mechanisms used to avoid necessary conflict:

   - "When the going gets tough, I'll withdraw into silence."

   - The self-deprecating, "I'll be negative about myself before anyone else can."

   - The enchanting approach: "I'll be so overly nice that people won't want to show anger toward me."

   - The Robin Williams strategy: "I'll use humor to cover up anything uncomfortable."

2. Defense mechanisms that divert any real responsibility away from yourself:

   - "Leave me alone, that's just the way I am."

- "That's not my job."

- "The ball's in their court. There's nothing I can do."

- "I hear only what I want to hear."

3. The most prevalent and destructive defense mechanisms are the aggressive ones:

   - Being in an attack/counterattack mode

   - Being critical of everything and everyone

   - Actively gossiping or going behind someone's back rather than being direct

4. And the greatest handmaiden to LeaderShock:

   - Needing to be right all the time

DEALING WITH OUR DEFENSE MECHANISMS

If you find yourself resonating with some of these behaviors, you're not alone. From time to time everyone finds defenses helpful as protection from something painful, but when they become automatic responses they no longer serve you well as a leader. Usually holdovers from the past, now they limit your choices, impede your responses and make it impossible to hear helpful feedback. In the end they keep you away from the healthy relationships and fresh ideas vital to effective leadership.

Is the goal to be free of all defenses? I've never run across anyone who is. They're a natural human response to vulnerability. However, one of the most compelling and irrefutable discoveries from my research is this: *Thriving leaders spend the least amount of time reacting defensively.*

Part of your liberation from LeaderShock is acknowledging that as your defensiveness decreases, your leadership effectiveness increases. Defensive conversations never work! They're like a greasy fast-food burger. The first few bites seem appealing but in the end all you've got is a stomachache. The results are always unsatisfying. And the mistrust at the heart of defensive positions supplants the trust on which successful relationships are built. Paradoxically, the best defense is to have *no* defense.

"I never saw an instance of one or two disputants convincing the other by argument."

—Thomas Jefferson

Considering that most of our defense mechanisms are ingrained behaviors and so many other people in the work environment are making excuses and pointing fingers, taking a nondefensive position might seem formidable.

The Defense Remedy

There are two surefire approaches that end up protecting you better than your defensiveness. Both require that you first understand which defensive behaviors consistently get in your way and then become acutely aware of times when you invoke them.

The first approach goes back to Rule 1. When you're aware of retreating into defensiveness, stop and search for a more honest, authentic response. State your Intentions.

Gretchen, an accounting supervisor for a large insurance company, describes how she uses an Intention statement to eliminate a common fear: "Oddly enough, I figured out that my most debilitating defense was wanting everyone to like me. Afraid of hurting people's feelings or having them think I wasn't a nice person, I avoided giving tough feedback. When I did give any, it was so sugarcoated my message was always lost. I justified it by believing that leaders who want to motivate people should always be positive.

"Learning about LeaderShock opened up my eyes. I still want to be liked and I think I always will, but now I'm careful not to use that need as a way of avoiding responsibility. What helps me deliver tough messages now is to preface them with my Intention. 'I want to give you some feedback to help you be the best you can be. As a manager, I owe it to you.' I realize I'm actually being kinder when I give people important information, even if it's negative. In reality, I'm probably even more likable."

The second approach to avoiding defensiveness is to simply stop talking and listen. Actively shift the conversation by inviting other people to expand their thoughts through comments like, "Tell me more." or "I really want to hear what you have to say." Contrary to popular belief, it's the listener in a conversation who holds the power, not the speaker. Hard to believe? Think about it. The speaker's tone, focus, and content are actually determined by the way you're listening. Think about how you would speak to a person with a hostile facial expression and aggressive physical stance versus someone showing you undivided attention. When you're listening solely to hear the other person you diffuse the defensiveness. What you'll get is:

- Deeper understanding of the issue beneath the words of attack or anger

- Better information, which can change your assumptions about what's going on

- More time to collect your thoughts

- The speaker's feeling that you value their point of view

Best of all, after you've listened, the other person is typically more willing to listen to you.

True listening is defense-free. It insists you *listen to hear and learn rather than to respond*, even when you don't like the message. Deep listening is not so much a skill as it is an attitude. Olympic skiers focus 100 percent of their attention to each second of the slalom course, never breaking concentration to consider what they might say after they cross the finish line. In much the same way, as an active listener you devote 100 percent of your attention to the other person without allowing your mind to race ahead to your answer. This is how you clear away assumptions and open the door to creating a more meaningful and effective dialogue.

Both approaches, sharing your real Intentions and active listening, are about owning what's true, rather than running from the issues. And it's the running away from the difficult and painful things that often keeps us in the clutches of LeaderShock.

WHO'S RESPONSIBLE FOR WHAT?

Thriving leaders ask themselves, "In what ways am I responsible to myself and to others?" And, "In what ways are these people responsible to me?"

But let your caution lights flash: One setup for LeaderShock is the belief that taking responsibility means being responsible for doing it all. The notion that a leader's job is to know-it-all, fix-it-all, solve-it-all will drag you down. This savior mentality is part of an old leadership paradigm that is no longer desirable—or even possible. If you see yourself as the white knight galloping in to save the day, stop. The self-sabotaging savior phenomenon is yet another route into LeaderShock.

So let go of it. A big part of your accountability to yourself is holding other people accountable for what they are supposed to do. Great leaders don't do for others what those people can and must do for themselves.

"Few things help an individual more than to place responsibility upon him and to let him know that you trust him."

—Booker T. Washington

WHEN EVERYONE OWNS IT ALL: CREATING AN ACCOUNTABLE CULTURE

So what happens if you work for a blame-centered organization? In truth, your peers may be a bunch of vicious, backstabbing grandstanders, and your boss an attacking, finger-wagging tyrant. Still, you have the power to design the culture you want for your own team. Regardless of what's going on in the rest of your company, you can build a team that owns it all just as much as you do.

Start by modeling the way. You set the atmosphere, mood, and tone for your team. Your department is a direct reflection of you. When you don't own it all you can bet your team members won't either. You can't just model behavior and hope your staff embraces your own-it-all attitude. Your role as leader requires that you become just as explicit about interpersonal behavior as you are about performance expectations.

Here's what Max, leader of one of the most functional departments I've seen, does. Watching Max at work, I could see without a doubt how one, clear, adamant rule works in such panoramic ways. "Everyone who works for me knows my cardinal rule, *no blame or excuses!* It simply isn't allowed. It's my hot button and everyone knows it. I don't punish people for making mistakes, but I deal with unaccountable behavior, including not owning mistakes, more aggressively than I do *any* other performance issue. We have a team agreement that we all resolutely enforce. Our mantra is: *Support, encouragement and respect will be embraced and celebrated. Gossip, backstabbing, and making excuses without suggesting solutions, will not be tolerated.*

"Make no mistake: My staff can come to me anytime to share concerns or just blow off steam, but they don't leave my office before we've transitioned to an accountable approach to moving forward. The result: We trust each other because we know it's all out in the open."

"Ninety-nine percent of the failures come from people who have the habit of making excuses."

—George Washington Carver

Holding others accountable, not just for work product but for their behaviors, is the key. When you're relentless in this pursuit, your colleagues will see that there's something significant going on in your department, even if they don't know what's causing it. They'll just see you've got a motivated, upbeat team that gets a lot done. As Max put it, "When other managers say to me, 'You're so lucky to have such good people. All I've got is a bunch of complainers!' I just smile and think to myself, 'Yeah, I know.'"

What Max knows is that when a department or team is dysfunctional, everyone on that team, including the leader, has colluded to make it that way. Certainly the aggressive complainers and backstabbers have. But so has the quietest person who doesn't appear to be directly involved. How? Chances are that person wasn't doing anything to make things better. Chances are the quiet one wasn't accountable enough to give the feedback others needed to hear.

So we've finally arrived at the answer to the dilemma posed at the beginning of the chapter! If you want to break organizational patterns and create a culture of accountability, do something extraordinary. Convert the question you must ask yourself into a query to your employees. "What's *my* part?" becomes "What's *your* part? What can *you* do to make things better?" *This* is what creates the accountable culture we all want.

"Nothing strengthens the judgment and quickens the conscience like individual responsibility."

—Elizabeth Cady Stanton
Founding President,
National Woman's Suffrage Association

By way of review, let's spend a moment integrating the first two rules of the LeaderShock program. As issues arise, first set your Intentions (attitude and behavior) and then own it all by determining appropriate responsibilities for yourself and your staff. Just as Intention defines how you want to be, the own-it-all approach puts you on a path to get it. Combine these rules and you understand that you have both the freedom to choose your Intentions and the responsibility to ensure they are acted upon.

> *"Freedom is only part of the story and half the truth. That is why I recommend that the Statue of Liberty on the East Coast be supplanted by a Statue of Responsibility on the West Coast."*
>
> —Victor Frankl,
> *Man's Search for Meaning*

You're poised to make great things happen, which evokes the next question: How will you marshal your limited resources to get it all done?

SUMMARY OF RULE TWO

LeaderShock Trap No. 2:
The Victim/Savior

When we feel victimized by circumstances, we assign blame to others and react defensively. At other times we take on too much responsibility and undermine our ability to get things done.

New Intentions

- I refuse to blame anyone or anything, especially myself. I understand that blame can only lead to frustration and stagnation. Instead, I ask "What's my part?" and use the answer to that question to move to a better place.

- I don't react defensively. I state my Intentions instead. During volatile conversations I diffuse unproductive conflict by listening to hear, not to respond.

- I create a department rule that blame, gossip, and finger-pointing in any form are prohibited. This does not include discussing bad feelings or relevant issues so long as that discussion concludes with owning it all.

3

REFUSE TO CONFORM

"To be no one but yourself in a world which is doing its best to make you just like everyone else, means to fight the greatest battle there is or ever will be."

—e e cummings

"How will I get everything done?" is one of the most frequent and most baffling questions managers ask. Overwhelmed by the sheer volume of work, the proliferation of meetings, and suffering from information overload, disheartened managers turn to the only solution modern business culture prescribes: Better time management! The grand illusion suggests it's all about better prioritizing of those meetings, better planning of the workflow, and better organizing of all that information. It isn't.

I've discovered thriving leaders working in some of the most demanding jobs, leaders who are nonetheless superbly productive, who feel fired up, and whose employees are veritable light bulbs of enthusiasm. How do they do it?

These leaders don't rely on techniques like time management but on something far more panoramic and effective. Their route to getting things done efficiently and effectively is to refuse to conform to the way everyone else leads or to pigeonhole their employees into set-in-stone job descriptions.

To follow their prescription, embrace this simple philosophy: Do what *you* love, then let others fill in the gaps by doing what *they* love. This is how you have the right people do the right things. It's all about capitalizing on strengths and passions rather than on capitulating to the "way it's done around here." Those strengths and passions are already there, and the time-starved leader who fails to tap them is reminiscent of a man going hungry at the banquet table.

After years of studying the behavioral choices of some of the happiest people on the face of the earth, I'm convinced it's virtually impossible to feel fulfilled if you don't spend your time doing what you love. In order to avoid the grips of LeaderShock even in the most conformist environments, emotionally buoyant leaders find a way to incorporate their individual passions. To them, "Doing what you love" is *not* a debatable issue. That may take creativity, sometimes unbridled imagination, but they all do it! In the final analysis, this is the drug that catapults leaders from ho-hum to exhilarated.

Put so simply, this seems obvious. Yet with the corporate requirement to "fit in," implementation may seem unlikely. Although corporations talk about embracing a diversity of thinking and approaches, many are actually more comfortable with a culture of sameness. As a result, conventional wisdom tells us it's safer, and therefore in our best interest, to do things in the accepted way and carefully portray the right image.

Not so. Politically correct leaders who try to fit in by using the latest buzzwords and taking on acceptable attributes are left in a curious dilemma. They may actually succeed in climbing the leadership ladder, but become more firmly entrenched in

LeaderShock with each rung they ascend. Why? *Blending in to avoid workplace conflict, ends up creating internal conflict.* These people are entrapped by a pronounced disconnect between who they really are and who the company pushes them to be. Becoming a corporate clone means ignoring invigorating and natural talents in favor of a tense façade. By trying to emulate their organization's most respected leaders, cloned managers are out of integrity with themselves, exhausted by looking over their shoulders, and hypervigilant about whether they're doing it right.

What they're doing is analogous to Laurence J. Peter's famous Peter Principle. He hypothesized that managers were promoted to their level of incompetence. Managers in the depths of Leadershock operate not by the Peter Principle, but by its close corollary, the "Paul" Principle: LeaderShocked managers rise only based on their façade. And at some point in their climb up the ladder the façade creates such inner tension and self-disconnection that they lose sight of their own well being and eventually tumble.

"Conformity is the enemy of thought and the jailer of freedom."

—John F. Kennedy

In my work, I encounter these lost souls every day. But the emotional and physical burnout I see in their eyes doesn't have to happen to you. To avoid the Paul Principle, you can learn how to balance a "do what you love" philosophy with corporate pressure to conform. But let's not be naïve about what you're up against. We've all witnessed people who are so busy doing their own thing that they seem to float, remaining disconnected from the day-to-day workings of the organization. There is, of course, a caveat: You can't just march to your own drummer without first doing something else. You have to work smart. That's where thriving leaders have devised a clever and essential approach.

THE SECRET TO DOING WHAT YOU LOVE

Maneuvering through the minefield of a company culture and emerging with your individuality intact requires two consecutive elements.

ELEMENT ONE: DEMONSTRATE COMPANY LOYALTY

Before anything else, thriving leaders enthusiastically embrace their company's culture by aligning themselves with the company's best characteristics. In a nutshell, to be able to do what *you* love, you have to first love something about the company. And that something may be any or all of the following—its values, vision, products, employees, or services.

Let's take a case in point. Dean, like other thriving leaders, believes there is no advantage to conformity. Five years ago, after joining a conservative financial services firm, he intentionally paved the way for his own passions to flourish. "When I first arrived in my new job, I made a decision to walk a mile in the company's shoes. I focused exclusively on the positives. I made it my goal to understand why things happened in certain ways and what made the system work. I sought out the long-time employees and asked questions. Slowly, from their answers I came to see the company's underlying values and learned to love those values. This allowed me to adopt an authentic sense of loyalty and pride in working for the organization. And, I did everything I could to state my devotion. Once everyone knew of my loyalty, I could take a tough stand and let my true opinion, style, and judgment come out."

Dean's approach worked and he's risen through the ranks. Recently he faced another test. The company president asked Dean to plan an aggressive global expansion from twenty-eight offices to forty-eight within 5 years. But Dean saw a problem. He felt the global brand identity needed revision before the company could grow so aggressively. Dean also knew that the brand identity had come from the president himself. Doing it *his* way meant challenging the president's cherished idea.

Actually, that's just what he did. Because Dean had previously demonstrated his loyalty to the president, Dean's unorthodox approach was received with open ears. Dean thrives on the freedom to say what he really believes because, as he says, "The company knows when I challenge it, I'm doing so entirely in the pursuit of wanting it to be better."

In Dean's case, he is so "value added" that the issue of conformity is not considered by senior managers. When it comes to the bottom line, healthy companies are much more excited by people who can think productivity and challenge the system than those who simply look the part.

"He who marches in rank and file has already earned my contempt. He has been given a large brain by mistake, since for him the spinal cord would suffice."

—Albert Einstein

ELEMENT TWO:
DEVELOP YOUR DIFFERENCES

Once your organizational loyalty is established, distinguish yourself as unique. Exhilarated and powerful leaders are ingenious about actively developing their differences, not hiding them. Let me be clear. This isn't the act of a solo revolutionary, and it's certainly not one of pushing others away. It's an attempt to deliberately express distinctiveness by vigorously engaging the favorite parts of yourself, including such specialized strengths as a vivid imagination, an adventurous spirit, or a charismatic personality. It's also about sharing your perceptions and opinions using your own vocabulary, preferring originality and authenticity to the catch phrase of the moment.

Why do these differences lead to personal success?

- Great motivators always have an authentic connection with those they motivate, and being yourself provides that point of genuine connection.

- When highly visible new projects are being considered, leaders with strong identifiable talents (not the vanilla, run-of-the-mill variety) leap to mind to play key roles.

- You feel relaxed and in control when you're in sync with yourself.

"To be what we are, and to become what we are capable of becoming, is the only end to life."

—Robert Louis Stevenson

IDENTIFYING YOUR PASSIONS

How do you bring the favorite parts of yourself to the job? Start by making a Personal Peaks list. These peaks are so named because, just like mountain tops, they rise above the ordinary landscape. Personal Peaks consist of two components:

- What you're especially good at (your peak talents)

- What you love to do (your peak passions)

Here's why both criteria must dovetail: Just because you're good at something (for me, math would qualify), doesn't mean you are passionate about it (as it happens, I get no thrills from math). We're looking for the confluence of the two.

Here's how to create your own Personal Peaks list. First, clear your mind. Don't think about your job description or related responsibilities. Just forget for a moment about all the things piled up on your desk. Focus on abilities, both large and small, that meet both criteria—your talents and passions. Don't censor, judge, or eliminate answers. Push yourself for honesty, and be sure to speak from your heart—don't get caught up in other people's formulas for success. Make this an act of sheer self-affirmation.

Let the Personal Peaks list be your professional compass. Keep the list ever present. When new assignments emerge, refer to that list, and instead of reverting to time-honored methods that don't tap your talents, use your imagination to determine how to approach the task in *your* way. This is what energizes you and makes you soar rather than bogging you down in workplace drudgery. There's a wisdom and a fierceness to applying the talents on your list to the things that need to get done, and those qualities are best illustrated by looking at leaders who've done so. Let's look at two.

A STAR IS BORN

Justin, twenty-eight years old, is an outgoing and creative leader at a midsized retail company. The sidebar contains some excerpts from Justin's Personal Peaks list.

JUSTIN'S PERSONAL PEAKS

- Being creative
- Performing
- Coaching employees
- Idea generation
- Seeing the big picture
- Using humor
- Spontaneity
- Making presentations
- Socializing with lots of people
- Opening up new options
- Infusing values or morals
- Working collaboratively, rather than alone
- Creating an optimistic environment
- Developing trusting relationships

When Justin was appointed head of the Customer Service department, he fell heir to a tenured staff of eighty phone representatives. This department of forty-something-year-olds had been managed for years by an apathetic and laissez-faire supervisor whom they exploited to the hilt. Because the department wasn't held accountable for results, performance had slipped. Justin was brought in to clean things up and as you can imagine, news of his arrival received about the same welcome as a case of the flu. "I knew I'd be fighting an uphill battle to gain credibility. *My sole Intention when I first got there was to connect to each person by exhibiting the best of me.*" (His Personal Peaks)

Tapping into his high-spirited personality, Justin would frequently make his way around the department, cubicle to cubicle, serving coffee and homemade pound cake, all the while checking in with each of his crew. Since his predecessor rarely left his office, reactions to Justin's unaccustomed visits were mixed at first. But with persistence, Justin began winning the department members over. With newfound respect, he proceeded to his second Intention: To upgrade the level of service in the department.

Justin created a skills assessment and began to deal aggressively with performance issues. It was clear there'd been little training to enhance skills, so he created a training program by using real-life cases gleaned from staff interviews. Bringing his own brand of humor and creativity —items of high priority on his Peaks list—to bear, he facilitated these sessions himself, parlaying customer-relations training into an event full of contests, prizes, and interactive exercises.

THE ORGANIZER

Justin's highly extroverted personality played into his success turning around the department. For equally impressive leaders though, this approach would be as appealing as dental surgery. Another leader, Jerry, is almost the polar opposite in personality, an introvert with a drive toward structure. "Just as fish are born to swim, I was born to organize," he says. Excerpts from Jerry's Personal Peaks list are shown in the sidebar.

JERRY'S PERSONAL PEAKS

- Organization of information
- Working one-on-one with people
- Developing loyalty with staff
- Establishing procedures
- Written communications
- Coordinating workflow
- Project management
- Solving puzzling problems

While Jerry's list shares nothing with Justin's, they did share a predicament. Jerry was selected to lead a troubled thirty-seven-person unit described by senior management as "a bunch of deadbeats." Like Justin, Jerry's initial Intention was to gain credibility. Shy and uncomfortable with the informality of management by walking around, he played to one of his strengths instead. Sequestering himself in his den at home one evening, he personalized a message to each employee on his monogrammed stationery. He pledged ongoing loyalty to every staff member by guaranteeing direct feedback. When training was sorely needed, Jerry developed a full curriculum of two-hour modules, complete with detailed leaders' guides for each course, then lined up guest speakers to do the training.

Two very different styles, both prized by their companies for getting results. The message in each case is the same: To stay out of LeaderShock, do it your way! Now you're ready to lead your staff to success using the same principle.

"It takes courage to grow-up and turn-out who you really are."

—e e cummings

CAPITALIZING ON YOUR PEOPLE'S PASSIONS

We've focused a lot of attention on the personal costs of ignoring your strengths. It's worth acknowledging that those aren't the only costs. One of the greatest losses for leaders who are overwhelmed and short on time is the failure to maximize the individual talents of their people.

Begin by debunking one of the cherished, yet failed, notions of leadership: That a leader's job is to develop people's weaknesses. Today the reverse is true. To move out of LeaderShock, zero in on the talents and strengths of your people and develop them to the hilt. Don't worry about fixing their weaknesses. Assigning people to tasks that don't play to a strength, or attempting to improve people by insisting that they put their energy in areas that don't come naturally, only adds to everyone's frustration, especially yours. Particularly in times of crisis, forget about developing people's deficits (that does not mean ignoring performance problems).

When was the last time you saw one of those professional development plans (that are all built around weaknesses) actually fix anything? Most of us aren't good at certain things and never will be.

That's why leaders who thrive have a surprisingly unconventional take on the concept of development plans. They develop individuals in a more affirming way: Rather than identifying a person's weakest qualities, they identify the strongest. Then, they encourage employees to develop those qualities until they evolve from a solid strength to an extraordinary talent.

"Too many people overvalue what they are not and undervalue what they are."

—Malcolm Forbes

Thriving leaders create a Peak list for everyone in their department, just as they did when they created such a list for themselves. When you put together project teams, be smart about it. Match the challenges and needs of the project to the talents on your team. Go beyond technical expertise to focus on the less obvious, but potentially more important talents such as a willingness to collaborate, creative idea generation, careful record keeping, and computer expertise. Your departmental Peak list will provide the roadmap to move your department forward in the most effective and efficient way.

> *"The same man cannot be skilled in everything; each has his special excellence."*
>
> —Euripides

UNCOVERING TALENTS

How do we determine people's strengths? The most obvious way is to ask employees to create their own Personal Peaks lists. But another way seems to work better. Be like a watch dog. As people go about their day, keep your eyes peeled to identify their special talents, valuable behaviors, and natural abilities.

Your Intention is to look for what you value in each employee, not what you don't. Consider Tom's approach: His Intention is to get the whole person, with full capabilities and goodwill, to walk through the office door each morning. Tom told me his story of being assigned to lead a troubled Operations department for a manufacturer. "There was plenty I could have criticized about the team but I started out looking only for the underlying strengths in each person," he recalled. As part of the deal he inherited the purchasing manager, Arlene. Nit-picky, noncollaborative, and suffering from poor relationships with her internal customers, Arlene was, nonetheless, a workhorse who did the job of three. As Tom related, "In spending more time with Arlene, I began to see she was excellent at detail and her objectionable perfectionism arose from an intense desire to do things well. I considered these leadership strengths."

Tom called Arlene in for a talk. Expressing praise for her remarkable level of commitment and the sheer volume of work she got done, Tom also described her attention to detail as a severely misdirected strength. "Arlene," he said, "I want to help you channel this wonderful attribute into something more productive and satisfying for everyone, especially you." Tom didn't pull any punches. He shared his observations about her drill sergeant management techniques and offputting urge to pin people down with comments like "But that isn't what you said last time!" Because these issues were presented in the context of enhancing professional strengths, Arlene put aside her usual defensiveness and the two began what was to become a successful collaboration for determining how to best use her much needed talents.

"Each citizen should play his part in the community according to his individual gifts."

—Plato

At this point, we've discussed three rules for triumphing over LeaderShock. First, actively set and state your Intentions. Second, own it all, rather than blame others or defend yourself. Third, as we've seen in this chapter, tap into your strengths and passions rather than doing things in the same way as everyone else. But if your leadership experience is fraught with bigger problems and traumas, this may all sound a little too easy. The next rule offers a new way of dealing with the inevitable stressors of leadership. Get ready to *Recast*.

SUMMARY OF RULE THREE

LeaderShock Trap No. 3:
The Company Conformist

We believe that it's safer to fit into the company's prescription for success. We do things in the acceptable ways even if they don't play to our strengths or those of our staff. And we slot people into jobs without tapping into their diversity of talents.

New Intentions

- I embrace my company's values without becoming a corporate clone. I actively develop my differences by capitalizing on my Personal Peaks—the things I'm both good at and love to do. I use these peaks to approach my leadership responsibilities.

- I look for what I value in each employee and focus on developing employees' strengths into extraordinary talents as opposed to trying to fix their weaknesses.

- I address heavy workloads by having the right people do the right things. To make this happen, I match my people's Personal Peaks to departmental needs.

4

RECAST STRESS INTO STRENGTH

"Adversity is the first path to truth."

—Lord Byron

Every leader knows that despite Herculean efforts things can go terribly wrong. Just when you least expect it, something explodes—a key employee quits and blames you, you're passed over for a promotion in favor of someone less qualified, the boss blows up after you lose a key account and fail to make your numbers. There's no way around the fact that the leadership role brings with it a certain amount of emotional pain and anxiety. Let's face it: The source of workplace stress is usually a people problem—the kind that wakes you up at 3 A.M. replaying yesterday's scenarios, imagining all the things you should have said then, and might have to say tomorrow.

The real question is *not* how to avoid stress, but how to deal with it head on. Prominent leaders agree on one remedy: Transform your greatest problems into precious assets.

"An optimist sees an opportunity in every calamity, a pessimist sees a calamity in every opportunity."
—Sir Winston Churchill

"When written in Chinese, the word "crisis" is composed of two characters. One represents danger, and the other represents opportunity."
—John F. Kennedy

"We are continually faced by great opportunities brilliantly disguised as insoluble problems."
—Lee Iococca

Most of us subscribe to the theory that problems can convert to opportunities. But how? Until now, no one has given leaders a practical roadmap to implement this idea. I have such a roadmap. I call it Recasting: The LeaderShock stress buster and one of most unique rules in the program. This single leadership behavior can change your life.

WHAT IS RECASTING?

Distinctly different from the concept of reframing, which entails shifting your perceptions to something positive, Recasting exploits problems for what they can teach you about what's not working and how to break ineffective patterns. It is at once efficient, surprising, and acutely analytical. Best of all, you often emerge having not only rid yourself of the problem but with something better than you had before the problem arrived.

Fundamental to the process is something thriving leaders are adamant about: Rather than deny an issue exists (by burying it, wishing it would go away, or just not talking about it), they engage it directly and honestly.

Recasting has three stages: emotions, meaning, and opportunities.

STAGE 1: EMOTIONS

Surprising but true, this business process starts with emotions and nothing but emotions. Even the most logical, no-nonsense leaders have learned that when they deal with stress-producing issues, their first question has to be, "How do I feel about this?" Here, "feel" means the real thing—angry, scared, hurt, sad, perhaps even happy. If you come up with answers like "Concerned" or "Surprised," try again. Go for the underlying emotions.

As you will learn, the first stage of Recasting is anything but touchy-feely. Rather, it's an analytical step critical to good business decisions. Skipping the emotions stage of Recasting is like trying to enter your house without opening the door. It doesn't work. Your emotional reactions are based on your professional experience and judgment and are primary indicators of what's truly happening. There's a wealth of information to be gathered simply by being attuned to your feelings. And besides, suppressing emotion is typically what causes the stress.

STAGE 2: MEANING

Next, the best leaders postpone fixing anything in order to take a discerning look at the reasons for the problem. The self-revealing questions they ask include

- What does it say about me that I have this problem—about my practices, my departmental policies, my relationship with customers and staff?

- What can I learn from this?

- How can I make this situation useful to me and my employees?

You're on shaky ground if you attempt to fix a problem without first understanding what it means to you and the organization. By looking for inherent meaning, you open a rich treasure chest of valuable gems that lead to new information, insight, and opportunities.

STAGE 3: OPPORTUNITIES

Not until you've understood how you feel (Stage 1) and the meaning surrounding the issue (Stage 2), are you prepared to explore Stage 3: Opportunities. Here you transform your learning into possible new approaches. You open the creative floodgates and ask,

"As a result of the problem, what are the new opportunities for me and my department?" Let your imagination flow. Examine every new idea and approach. Only then are you adequately armed to make informed decisions to fix a big problem. (Remember, quick fixes are reserved for small, everyday issues.)

Ultimately, Recasting guides leaders through even the most traumatic situations by unearthing the golden nuggets of growth and insight they contain. Recasting becomes your tool to look at things differently: To know that you don't have to live with stress and that learning from painful events can be productive, creative, and ultimately, exhilarating! As you'll see in the remainder of this discussion of Rule 4, Recasting is a process that any leader can use to address three troubling types of issues—personal work stress, a team or entire company with tough issues, and even a community confronted with a crisis. Let's turn to an example.

RECASTING PERSONAL WORK STRESS: BETRAYAL ON THE JOB

Elena, Product Development Supervisor of a chemical company, applied not only Recasting during a personally painful episode, but also the other three leadership rules we've learned so far. Elena attended an offsite conference with Todd, the get-ahead-at-all-costs, politically savvy new V.P. of Marketing. The event seemed unremarkable to Elena. But upon her return to the office she was stunned to learn that Todd had widely reported that she drank excessively at the conference and misrepresented the company. Neither of his claims were true but because of Todd's close relationship to the president, she feared that Todd's words would have more credibility than her own. That night Elena was haunted by all the worst possibilities, the most scary being that she'd be fired.

I know Elena well. She's high on integrity and professionalism, a sharp analyst, and a self-motivated leader. Driven to solve the problem immediately, Elena was stumped. All the fixes she contemplated offered dubious results because they were defensive postures. She considered and then rejected persuading others that Todd's allegations weren't true. She discounted the idea of keeping her head down until everything blew over. And quitting to look for a new job wasn't what she wanted either. Having recently attended a LeaderShock seminar, Elena decided instead to call on her Recasting skills.

STAGE 1: EMOTIONS

Elena tends to be a thinker, not a feeler, so she really pushed herself to focus solely on her feelings—an uncomfortable place for her to be. How *did* she feel? Her answer: Not just angry, but furious, taken advantage of and violated! And maybe above all, frightened about her job security.

STAGE 2: MEANING

Elena segued to asking "What does this predicament say about me? What does it all mean?" After taking a hard look at the situation and her role in it, new understanding emerged. Her initial insight was the realization that she was allowing one person (and not a person of integrity) to damage her reputation and stellar work record. As a result, Elena set an Intention to take hold of her power. Rather than blame Todd, which would have been easy to do, she took the high road and focused exclusively on the question "What's my part?" (See Rule 2 for more details on this.)

Elena's inquiry prompted further exploration and new questions about what it all meant. "Why did Todd's word have more credibility than mine? Am I adequately valued in this company? Are my strengths being used? Do I feel fulfilled in my work?" Elena concluded that she was being neglected and suddenly began to understand why. She'd been complacent. She wasn't selling her talents, highlighting her accomplishments or making herself visible.

STAGE 3: OPPORTUNITIES

What were the opportunities? Turning an episode this distasteful into an opportunity seems inconceivable. Nonetheless, after completing Stage 2, Elena came up with opportunities that did more than just eliminate the problem; they turned her career around. She saw this as a chance to deal with some long-standing concerns. With her behavioral strategy in place, she went to see Marta, her boss. Elena shared her Intentions to both respond nondefensively and address gnawing career issues.

Impressed by her accountable and professional response to a messy situation, Marta, accompanied by Elena, paid Todd a visit. Even though Todd denied the matter and cleverly avoided an apology, things were resolved. Marta also cleared things up with the company's president and Elena felt relieved. With the initial issue behind her, Elena was ready to repair her overlooked career. She energetically began opening doors to spotlight her talents. Volunteering to make a presentation for prospective new clients garnered positive attention from the Sales Manager. After a career-focused lunch with him the following week, Elena was appointed to a prominent new task force. And as a grand finale to the story, 4 months later Todd mysteriously left the company.

When you find yourself in a situation like Elena's, the natural tendency is to turn inward.

Some of the most effective leaders I know who normally reach out easily to customers and employees, withdraw and internalize when it comes to dealing with their own work-related stress. Believing that a real leader should be stoic and capable of handling any issue alone is a LeaderShock trap. You've heard the adage, "Don't die alone in your bunker!" Well, don't! Every leader needs support. One of the beauties of Recasting is that you can use the process for engaging other people in your bunker to help you deal with the things that keep you up at night.

Pull a few people, your best support network, together and ask for help. Walk through each of the Recasting steps. Tell them how you feel and the impact of the problem on you. Solicit their ideas about the meaning of the problem and then ask them to brainstorm new opportunities and approaches.

Regardless of the issue, this group process works, and sometimes with surprising results. In fact, it's not uncommon for the Recasting partner who knows your job least to infuse a blast of energy into the proceedings by coming up with the most creative and practical ideas. By encouraging your colleagues to unleash their collective brainpower and share their perspectives, you'll often walk away with a fresh mental picture. You may also find that you:

- Relieve your anxiety altogether.

- Get affirmation for the ideas you've already come up with or find relief by simply being able to talk out loud about them.

- Receive ongoing support from your Recasting mates because now they clearly understand what you're up against. You might be surprised to learn that they are secretly dealing with the same things.

TEAM RECASTING

It's exciting to see great leaders aggressively manage group learning through team Recasting sessions. Leaders first create a candid environment by encouraging the real issues to surface. Getting problems on the table in organizational cultures where failure is hidden or punished might initially feel like trying to swim upstream. Creating a Recasting-positive culture requires some preliminary steps.

The swiftest way to foster culture change is through cues you give about how people should behave. As a prelude to Team Recasting sessions, it's crucial to set behavioral norms. Admit mistakes to your staff so they'll have a model for doing the same to you. Talk about ways you were instrumental in things that *didn't* go well. Further, set the stage by building in Intention statements. Tell your team that you encourage candid disclosure of errors and concerns and that disclosures will be used for learning, not for punishment. Then get the most critical issue out in the open.

With the issue fully exposed, you're poised to follow the three stages of Recasting, adapted for use by a group. First get *everyone's* emotions out on the table. (It's crucial that you enforce a no-blame-no-gripe policy during this stage). Next, analyze the meaning of the problem, and then brainstorm new opportunities and approaches. The following story illustrates how an entire company chose to Recast.

FINANCIAL CATASTROPHE STRIKES

When catastrophic problems threaten everyone's livelihood, companies are well served by engaging their leaders in Recasting. This was the case several years ago during an intensive 5-day LeaderShock seminar I was leading for the fifteen division heads of a high-tech company with about 800 employees. The organization had been hit hard by new competition in a declining economy. Each seminar participant reported to one of the five executive leaders and all had multiple layers of staff reporting to them.

On the fourth day, I received an urgent message from the president: First quarter numbers had just come in. Although they'd hoped for a turnaround is sales, numbers had precipitously declined to a dramatic low.

When I called him back he pleaded, "Please don't mention anything about this to the group. I don't want to upset them until I have to." I disagreed. If there was ever an opportunity to deal openly with a company-wide crisis, this was it! I asked if he and the rest of the executive group would drop everything and drive down to the conference center.

After lunch, the participants were greeted by the president and executive team who presented the sobering numbers. The group was stunned. When standard operating procedure would have been to immediately begin problem solving, we didn't. With no philosophizing, analysis, or resolutions permitted, I asked each seminar participant to share only real feelings about what had just been announced. What surfaced was a cornucopia—anger, blame, frustration, even, from one person, happiness that the company had finally hit rock bottom and would now take drastic steps. From the responses we realized that everyone was unquestioningly committed to making a turnaround work. This adrenaline pumped room was ready for Stage 2.

In Stage 2, I led a group discussion spurred by the question: "What does it say about us and our organization that we have this monumental problem?" The analysis left no stone unturned. Here were just a few of their revelations:

- If we're caught this much off guard by the numbers, we don't have functional financial systems in place.

- Efforts we've been making aren't working. We have to do something dramatically different.

- We've been in denial. We just keep performing the routine duties prescribed by our job descriptions as the company falls apart right before our eyes.

The results of these first two stages informed everything they would do for the ensuing 2 months. We can only speculate on what might have happened without their acute level of analysis and team involvement. Most likely their course of action would have been less befitting the severity and scope of the situation.

Now we were poised to look at possibilities for forging ahead. Our brainstorming centered on imaginative ways of identifying new short-term roles for everyone, ways to quickly shift priorities, and ways to hold one another accountable.

As we ended our discussion, there were still no solutions to increase revenue, but the team was poised to attack the problem with a fresh backdrop, and they were jazzed about getting started. On Monday morning all previously established ways of doing things ceased. Abandoning their normal job functions, leaders instituted a daily morning meeting. They gave themselves over to the war-room atmosphere of a ferocious political campaign. Minute to minute they monitored daily income data, used swat teams to rally employees around productive activities, and held themselves accountable for every action. In the crisis came unity and spirit. Nobody pursued business as usual. The I.T. manager got out from behind her computer and began calling new prospects. The manufacturing manager hit the streets to follow up on sales leads. The result? Everyone chipped in with a crackling energy not experienced for way too long. Each person became instrumental in saving the company. This organization not only survived (by the skin of its teeth), but now, a year later, is inching toward financial health. The heroes? Every single leader.

"Show me a hero, and I'll show you a tragedy."

—F. Scott Fitzgerald

When you consistently use the Recasting process with your people you'll make profound changes in your organizational culture. You'll create an environment where people feel safe to bring up bad news, that is free of negative judgment and blame, and where people are rewarded for candor. That's why thriving leaders these days are spending less time in production meetings rehashing what's going well, and more time recasting failures and disappointments to ensure future success.

RECASTING ON A GRAND SCALE

Even though this book is dedicated to analyzing unsung leaders rather than the rich and famous, there is a powerful example of a leader who reached folkloric status by guiding an entire city, and ultimately a nation, through the Recasting process. In 2001, then Mayor of New York City, Rudy Giuliani, followed each Recasting stage (whether he had a name for it or not) when he faced one of the greatest traumas in American history. In less than 4 months, he catapulted himself from a lowly 32 percent approval rating to *Time Magazine*'s Person of the Year. Just prior to 9/11, Giuliani had been a media target for his controversial lifestyle and divisive politics, but by year end *Time* was praising him as a "global symbol of healing and defiance" and "the greatest mayor in the city's history."

Regardless of how any of us might view his politics, it's worthwhile to dissect his remarkable Recasting odyssey. Immediately after the twin towers fell, Giuliani made a pivotal move. Employing the feeling stage of Recasting, he decided that New Yorkers "needed to hear from my heart." He led, not by strategizing behind closed doors, but by publicly exhibiting his grief and inspiring the city with an emotional Intention statement. "We are going to rebuild," he announced, "we're going to be stronger than we were before . . . I want the people of New York to be an example to the rest of the country and the rest of the world, that terrorism can't stop us."

Like any good Intention, this was a clear declaration of personal desire and motivation. Giuliani was not afraid to publicly state his personal feelings. "The number of casualties will be more than any of us can bear."

For a man who up until this point had been seen as a rigid, unfeeling, no-nonsense politician, this was a striking turnaround. In the weeks that followed, Giuliani devoted most of his time tending to the *emotions of the city*, appearing at more than 200 wakes, memorials, and funerals, and giving eulogies at many. In these eulogies he inspired survivors with his feelings about honor, sacrifice, and loss. These appearances were also the vehicle for his personal Recasting of the trauma. "I realized that one of the ways I could get through this is by going to the (memorial) services. They're heartbreaking but inspirational."

Without a doubt, the most important step he took in his meteoric rise to hero status was to unabashedly reveal his humanity. Giuliani's feelings provided a powerful medium around which the feelings of all New Yorkers could coalesce although at the time running from them would have felt easier and safer. Herein lies a dramatic example of why, during the really tough times, leaders must *never* skip the emotions stage. Although countercultural for most men *and* women, particularly during times of trauma, thriving leaders consider it their responsibility to be courageous enough to state how they feel.

Though Stage 1 is my focus here, for the sake of completeness, let's follow through with Giuliani's other two Recasting stages:

- Stage 2: Giuliani looked for meaning, saying, "Maybe the purpose of all this is to
  find out if America today is as strong as
  when we fought for independence or when
  we fought for ourselves as a Union to end
  slavery or as strong as our fathers and

grandfathers who fought to rid the world of Nazism." Again, his own search for meaning was a model for the search of millions of people.

- Stage 3: What were the opportunities? Rudolph Giuliani pushed hard to reopen New York and urged everyone to get back to their lives, bringing together civic and business leaders to get people working together to move forward. He became a beacon of strength showing up everywhere pushing his message and sharing his thoughts about newfound opportunities.

Again, whether or not you agree with Giuliani's politics, it's undeniable that each Recasting step was critical to his personal success. Each step was also critical to the people of New York who needed a hero capable of guiding them through the trauma and addressing all their fears.

"High sentiments always win in the end. The leaders who offer blood, toil, tears and sweat always get more out of their followers than those who offer safety."

—George Orwell

I offer this Recasting process to leaders everywhere. I've used it with clients for small interpersonal issues and for the very biggest traumas like unexpected mergers, bankruptcy, and the effects of 9/11. And I will use it for those that will inevitably come in the future. So can you. When you find yourself awake at 3 A.M. worrying, let Recasting be your guide. Understand that you have a roadmap out. Think about how you will implement each stage and then go back to sleep.

SUMMARY OF RULE FOUR

LeaderShock Trap No. 4:
The Quick-Fixer/Denier

When we're hit with a stressful problem, we either apply a quick but ineffectual Band-Aid to the situation, or try to sweep it under the rug.

New Intentions

- I will deal with stressful issues head on. I understand that my best course of action is to invest time upfront engaging in the Recasting process.

- I Recast by following these three stages:

  - Explore my emotions and let them be my guide

  - Find the meaning and lessons inherent in the problem

  - Open up new opportunities and approaches without locking into simplistic solutions

5

REPLACE PLANS
WITH POSSIBILITIES

---

*"Whatever is flexible . . . will grow; whatever
is rigid and blocked will wither and die."*

—Lao Tzu

Rule 5 can best be illustrated by two equations:

$$Rigidity = LeaderShock$$
$$and$$
$$Flexibility = Leadership$$

In terms of their immediate impact on you, consider two more equations:

$$Rigidity = Disappointment$$
$$and$$
$$Flexibility = Exhilaration$$

In this era of widespread LeaderShock, the Rigidity Trap is everywhere. Why do we become unbending in our beliefs and why are our plans seemingly etched in stone? The causes are three-fold. First, the business environment is Process-Mapped, Palm-Piloted, and Day-Planned to death. Our every move is prescheduled, preapproved, systematized, and routinized. Second, there's the insecurity of our topsy-turvy economic climate, which makes us long for the comfort and security of the time-honored ways of doing things. And finally, we tend to look for one, simple answer to solve major struggles: "If I just visit each client more than once a month our business will grow." "If I can just hire two more people we'll reach our goals." "If I just had a better boss, I'd be happy at work." Unfortunately, by locking into rigid assumptions like these we rarely achieve what we want.

In striking contrast to this locked-down world, the most effective, invigorated leaders have an uncanny capacity to break out of the airtight container of formulaic business practices. They rebel against the urge to find simple, one-way solutions and instead open themselves to multiple possibilities for getting where they want to go. Their comfort and security come not from subscribing to a hard and fast plan but from relying on innovation and creativity as the natural tool for adapting and responding to the realities of the ever-changing world in which they work.

"If you don't change directions you're likely to end up where you were headed."

—Confucius

Chances are you've been in this invigorating place, too. If you look back on your own life to a time when you did something that was not merely good, but genuinely great, you'll find invaluable information. It's likely you didn't know at the start how wonderfully things would unfold. Rather, those instances of greatness were generated by character-

istics you brought to the event: inspired spontaneity, personal energy, and a willingness to adjust, create, and reshape along the way. You can bring these
same flexible characteristics to your work life, with
the same thrilling results.

TWO TYPES OF THINKING

Let's use a fishing trip as an analogy to understand
how a leader might achieve productivity in the
uncharted and ever-changing waters of business. In
approaching any decision, you can use two types of
thinking. The first is convergent thinking, which
quickly homes in, or converges, on just one way to
get to a solution. If you use convergent thinking on
your fishing trip, you plop yourself down on your
favorite end of the pier and, (1) identify the specific
fish you want to catch, (2) drop a single line into the
water, (3) determine precisely the proper depth, and
(4) sit back and wait to hook the big one. You might
have to wait a long time and you might not succeed
at all. Because you strictly adhere to your plan, the
one specific fish that has to come along at the predetermined depth might never arrive. You might
know exactly what you want but your approach has
limited in advance the possibility of success. Unfor-

tunately, you fail to optimize the marine circus swimming just out of reach of your single hook.

The second approach offers far more potential. It uses *divergent* thinking, a technique that shoots for many prospects. Fishing divergently, you toss out a net without a specific fish in mind. With such vast coverage, you're bound to land something that meets your needs. Sorting through the resulting catch, you choose which fish to keep and which to toss back. The considerable catch gives you a lot of material to work with. Now that you've first diverged, you can begin the process of elimination, until you arrive at a set of elements that offers the richest business outcome.

The wisdom of divergent thinking is the choice of thriving leaders. They strive to generate a host of novel and productive options, and then converge on the best final result. Thriving leaders know that by failing to review a wide enough range of options before making their decision they risk two unfortunate outcomes:

- They choose too quickly and then hang rigidly onto what proves to be a poor decision, or

- As things continue to go awry they panic, begin to bounce from one rushed solution to another, and time after time lock into another new plan.

The all too common LeaderShock cry, "Forget what I said before, now we're going to do it this way" is the hallmark of a leader trapped in the "game plan du jour syndrome." This unnecessary behavior is a source of great consternation for the employees who become the rigid leader's unwitting victims.

Leaders with the drive and energy to explore many options begin with a far better, well thought out decision, then stay open as they implement it, modifying and adapting it as new information becomes available. Maria learned how to become just such a manager. She saved both her career and her sanity by metamorphosing from a perennially convergent thinker to a productively divergent one.

"The best way to have a good idea is to have lots of ideas."

— Nobel laureate Linus Pauling

COMING UP FOR AIR

Maria had been one of her company's best employees—smart, effective, a can do person, well liked by managers and colleagues. Promoted to the head of her four-person department, she was responsible for meeting aggressive departmental goals. She conscientiously tried to stay on top of things, as she once had when she was an individual contributor. And, Maria was sure she knew best. But while she was rigidly adhering to time-tested ways of doing things and monitoring her staff to make sure they were doing things right, the department fell further and further behind. Her most frequent statement to staff was "We have no time to explore new ways of working." Once viewed as positive and dynamic, Maria was now seen as callous and she was universally disliked.

By the time I met Maria, she was distraught and ready to quit, as was everyone else on her frustrated team. I'm happy to say she's now back on track—more than anything else, because she realized she'd fallen into the rigidity trap.

Following her graduation from the Leader-Shock program, she held a bold and unorthodox meeting with both employees *and* peers. When all had gathered in the conference room, Maria made a heartfelt Intention statement. "I've had an epiphany. As a new manager, I've been overly controlling and unyielding with all of you when I needed to be inclusive and creative. I apologize. I need your support in helping me take a more collaborative approach."

Since all four members of Maria's department were twenty-somethings, she felt that their educational backgrounds and natural acceptance of flexible team assignments would make them enthusiastic. But as hungry as they were to use their creativity, Maria's announcement was initially met with skepticism. "You can't teach an old dog new tricks" was their attitude. So to positively and aggressively live up to her declaration, Maria implemented a number of changes to build a more inclusive, playful environment. Rather than checking up on people to ensure they were doing it *her* way, she led staff Recasting sessions. She listened more and engaged individuals in lively brainstorming interchanges that were full of ideas and suggestions. In meetings they played the "what if" game (for example, "What if we measured sales by customer, not by department").

The group was beginning to believe that Maria really was able to change. Meanwhile, Maria, an orderly, tidy person by nature, still needed structure and constantly fought a battle with the rigidity demons. But she found that the more she engaged her people in creative thinking, the harder they seemed to work. And everybody was having so much more fun, especially Maria. As time went on there was no question that the department had not only regained productivity, it had surpassed its previous performance.

A NEW KIND
OF STRATEGY

Historically, leaders have been told, "The key to success is having a solid strategic plan supported by specific, measurable, attainable, and realistic action plans." In today's world, this thinking is pure folly. *Measurable strategies are actually tactical plans.* These metrics-driven, ritualistic documents emphasize benchmarks, focus on predetermined numbers and prescribe fixed actions that we *believe* will deliver desired outcomes. Because they rely on what we already know as a way to predict what needs to be done in the future, they limit us before we've even begun. Although the plan might have made perfect sense when we established it, things are changing almost before the ink is dry: there's a different market, different customers, and different resources. It's no wonder that such a tiny proportion of these expensive and laboriously designed strategic plans are actually fully implemented.

What's the answer? Whether we're dealing with an entire company or an individual department, we need to be sure we're really talking about strategy, not tactics. Strategies are inherently flexible, long term, multifaceted, and big picture. They focus on outcomes like growth and profit rather than specifically measurable goals, and encourage directionality rather than prescribing a single path to success. To be a thriving leader we fundamentally change ourselves into strategic thinkers, rather than tactical planners. And we don't lock into any kind of process document. Our motto becomes: *Focused, but flexible.* We embark on a process of discovery. Every minute of every day we open up possibilities that will help us achieve our long-term goals. We don't just commit to three ways to get there, or five, or seven; we prospect for profitable opportunities all the time—during discussions with clients, conversations with competitors and in brainstorming sessions with the staff.

To stay out of LeaderShock you're constantly creating new strategies and adjusting old ones. You're responding to the day-to-day changes in your business environment and at the same time tweaking the long-term big picture as your situation changes. In this way you stay flexible in the short term *and* have a long-term notion of your desired outcomes that is resilient and based in the immediate realities of your economic world. As the old strategic plan collects dust on the bookshelf, you and your team feel energized and full of hope as you move in sync with the living and breathing organization in which you work.

OFFERING HOPE

I believe all leaders have an obligation to offer hope, not just to themselves but to their people as well. If you think about a time in your own life when you felt hopeless, it was probably because you felt cornered and believed you didn't have options. You were trapped, resigned, with no way out.

> *"Become a possibilitarian. No matter how dark things seem to be or actually are, raise your sights and see possibilities —always see them, for they're always there."*
>
> —Norman Vincent Peale

There's only one formula for overcoming hopelessness. It demands steadfastly creating a multitude of scenarios to move through roadblocks. Put simply, hope is born from believing there are options. Thriving leaders have scenarios to deal with specific business impediments, dynamic plans to create new markets, back pocket schemes for emergencies, blueprints for creating career paths for themselves and their employees. And when things reach rock bottom and seem intractable, they're like a wrestler pinned into a scissor lock by the opponent's brute force. With ingenuity, physical fluidity, and creative intelligence they finesse an opening and escape. *They find a way out of a "no way" situation.*

NEVER SAY DIE

A former Human Resources manager, Erin had to find a way out of "no way!" She'd been transferred from her beloved New York to assume the role of marketing manager in the Los Angeles branch of her property and casualty insurance company. Knowing no one in L.A. and little about marketing, she was ready for the adventure of her life when she eagerly faced her new boss.

Eugene was a LeaderShocked branch manager if ever there was one. Rigid as steel, he commanded, "There's only one way to do this job. Hit the road and visit our brokers. I want you in their offices 95 percent of the time. The rest of the time be on the freeway. That's your only role, educating them about our products."

Erin's hopes for developing a dynamic new career were dashed. She'd pictured an exciting opportunity to parlay her human relations skills into branch marketing. But Eugene's decree would have her driving to remote parts of L.A. and battling bumper-to-bumper Southern California traffic all to perform a single function. It felt like a jail sentence. As a strong extrovert she felt deadened at the thought of engaging in an endless series of one-on-one meetings. Hopelessness set in.

Superb at multitasking and developing training programs, she had always enjoyed a flair for design and loved being in the spotlight. In desperation she thought, "There's got to be a better way to do this job. I've got to figure out how to gain credibility by capitalizing on who I am, and not be forced to be someone I'm not."

To find that opportunity Erin began interviewing clients to discover how brokers think, what they need, and what motivates them to strike a deal. Her research became a far-reaching brainstorming marathon that ultimately uncovered scores of creative and stimulating ideas. Finally, she landed on an idea that fully resonated, a Products Fair for the brokers held right in the branch office. This wouldn't be a tired dog and pony show marred by stale presentations and the customary cheese and crackers, but an elegant extravaganza with fine wines, gourmet foods, professional displays, experts on hand to talk about each of the company's specialized insurance coverages, and exquisite giveaways. This event would both enlighten and motivate the branch's brokers, and could help them keep customers and attract new ones by learning about the full array of available services. Erin knew it would work, and best of all, this event would tap into every one of her talents.

All the research and planning prepared her to talk with the boss. Setting an Intention to be truthful, but to check her ego at the door, Erin began. "I've been thinking about what you said, Eugene—that my job is to educate our brokers. And I think I've come up with a fresh approach." Showing the boss that she could resourcefully reallocate money previously budgeted for travel, entertainment expenses, and marketing brochures, Erin was able to demonstrate that the event could be funded without draining an already tight expense plan. She got the OK.

Attended by the top brass from the home office, Erin's Products Fair was a glittering occasion that became a model for other branches in the company. Erin glowed with secret pride as attending agents congratulated Eugene on the success of the fair.

This is flexible thinking at work. When we begin with assumptions like "I'll never change my boss's mind," or, "There's only one way to do this," or, "It's not worth asking," we get lost in the rigid thought processes of LeaderShock. As Erin's story demonstrates, an investment of creativity upfront can save endless hours of toil, frustration, and unhappiness.

> *"I think and think for months and years. Ninety-nine times, the conclusion is false. The hundredth time, I am right."*
>
> —Albert Einstein

As we conclude this chapter, I want to offer a cautionary note. Some leaders are so aware of their problems with rigidity that they've made the mistake of swinging to another extreme. Believing that a complete lack of preconceived notions, a blank slate, lets them respond faster to upcoming changes, they invite chaos, which only intensifies LeaderShock. These leaders' people end up feeling scattered and frustrated. There's nothing sustainable to latch onto.

Chaos is not the opposite of rigidity. Healthy flexibility is where you want to be, inviting unexpected options and discovering new possibilities before making any final decisions. If life is indeed a journey, we as leaders would be wise to pay more attention to the odyssey and less to the final destination toward which we're headed.

> *"The afternoon knows what the morning never suspected."*
>
> —Swedish proverb

SUMMARY OF RULE FIVE

LeaderShock Trap No. 5:
The Rigid Controller

In our desire for security we lock into either the time-honored ways of doing things or a single-outcome plan to get what we want. This rigidity can lead only to disappointment and ineffectiveness in an ever-changing world.

New Intentions

- I'm a divergent thinker. I open up a multitude of options before I converge on a well thought out decision that I continually modify and adapt as I uncover new information.

- I'm a strategic thinker, not a tactical planner. I establish a clear, focused direction or strategy for my department but then do not limit myself with highly measured action plans. Rather, I embark on a process of discovery, continually searching for every possibility to realize my strategy.

- I offer hope when things seem hopeless. My Intention is to get beyond either company- or self-imposed boundaries and provide my people with new options. I resolutely find a way out of "no way."

6

FOCUS ON YOUR PEOPLE FIRST

"The ear of the leader must ring with the voices of the people."

—Woodrow Wilson

The devoutly held belief that customers come first turns out to be one of the most surprising LeaderShock traps. Rule 6 replaces conventional wisdom with this basic premise: *Focus on your people before anything else. When you take care of them, they take care of the customers.* And when you don't, they disengage and you're left with even more pressure on your shoulders. Imagine what would happen if the conductor of a symphony orchestra, in an earnest desire to please the paying public, turned around and conducted the concerto while facing the audience leaving the hard-working musicians to fend for themselves.

This doesn't suggest that you're constantly interacting with your people. It doesn't even mean that you devote most of your time to them. It means that over time the people who work for you become your big-picture priority. They have the highest place of honor reserved on your radar screen.

But how do you make your people a priority when there are so many other things that demand immediate attention? Most leaders fancy the notion of giving more attention to their people but can't put it into practice. "I'm too buried in other emergencies!" they tell me. My response is always the same, "If you want to get out of LeaderShock, you don't have time *not* to do this."

Complex theories abound that instruct leaders how to manage their people. And, since no two people and no two organizations are alike, choosing the right course is complicated. But in the tumultuous realm of LeaderShock simplicity is the name of the game. After sifting through countless leadership ideologies-of-the-month and distilling my own observations, I've come to understand something universal and timeless. Great people management boils down to discovering the answers to three potently affirming questions for *each* employee:

- What do you need?

- What motivates you?

- How can I show you I care?

Understand the unique answers to these questions, then respond to what you learn, and your people will know they come first!

QUESTION NO. 1: WHAT DO YOU NEED?

I believe your job, at its most elemental level, is to figure out what your employees need and then to give it to them. If you're not sure, ask! Even if you think you're sure, ask.

Molly, a supervisor at a petrochemical company, is blessed with a talent for getting to the heart of the matter. "The two questions I'm constantly asking my employees are composed of four little words, 'What do you need?' and 'How can I help?'" she says. "I make a deal with my people. I'll keep asking them what they need as long as they're prepared to hear 'No' when I honestly can't deliver. I can at least help brainstorm solutions or act as a sounding board to bounce ideas off or provide support. I don't solve my employees' problems, but they know I'm in their corner. Helping my staff is one of the great joys of my job."

Be like Molly and become the department sleuth. Block out an hour on your calendar just like you would for a scheduled meeting. Spend the time with your people asking straightforward and unsophisticated questions, "How's it going?" "What are you seeing out in the marketplace?" "What are customers saying?" "Are you getting the support you need?" By spending the hour listening to the voice of your people you'll gain far more valuable information than you would by attending any meeting.

Molly sees herself as an obstacle exterminator. In addition to her direct line of questioning, she relies on creative methods for uncovering employee roadblocks. The first of these is what she calls the

Happiness Meter. It requires polling each employee with the question, "On a scale of 1 to 10, if 1 means miserable and 10 means ecstatic, how do you rate yourself right now at work?" Regardless of the answer, she presses for specifics as to what it would take to move a 6 to a 7, or even a 9 to a 10. Molly's enthusiastic "How can I make you happier today?" is one of the standard queries to her thirty employees.

"What do you need?" is your opening, but you need to dig deeper. If employees are your greatest asset, then you'd better understand not only their needs but also what drives them.

> *"If you want one year of prosperity, grow grain. If you want ten years of prosperity, grow trees. If you want one hundred years of prosperity, grow people."*
>
> —Chinese Proverb

QUESTION NO. 2: WHAT MOTIVATES YOU?

Leaders who excel at managing people know that the answer to what motivates human beings cannot be found in a generic laundry list of techniques. Beware of titles like "Twenty Tips for Motivating Employees." People aren't generic. There are huge variations among us: I've noticed that many people are motivated by public acknowledgment of their contributions, but at least some feel embarrassed by the attention. Even though most of us feel inspired and invigorated by being part of a harmonious team environment, some prefer to work alone. Although most people are charged up by lots of time and attention from the leader, some don't like to be singled out. And even though salary and bonus are important, for some, money has little bearing on their level of motivation.

One statement, however, embodies the motivations of *every* person I've ever coached, trained, or managed. It is this: *Human beings want to feel worthwhile, valued, and respected.* These are universal desires.

"Everyone has an invisible sign hanging from his neck saying Make Me Feel Important! Never forget this message when working with people."

—Mary Kay Ash

Convert this understanding into a primary Intention: *I intend to figure out what makes each person feel important.*

You individualize your interactions according to what makes each person feel good about himself or herself. When you figure out what people most value about themselves, your job is to find ways to value that trait in them, too. Herein lies the key to generating extraordinary motivation.

"I tried to treat them like me, and some of them weren't."

—Coach Bill Russell

Kathryn, the owner of a West Coast design firm, makes it her goal to bring out the light in everyone, so she motivates her staff with an eye to igniting the spark within. Just as a detective looks for clues to solve a crime, Kathryn looks for clues to unravel the secret of each individual's unique motivator. "I know that Ali wants to feel competent." she relates. "His eyes light up whenever I say, 'Ali, I need your brain on this project.' or 'That sure was a smart thing to do!'" Kathryn also knows that Sophie, her staff assistant, feels important when she's given visibility. That's why Kathryn looks for every opportunity for Sophie to interface with other managers and why Kathryn has Sophie prepare and deliver the status report at monthly department meetings.

> *"Treat people as if they were what they ought to be, and you help them to become what they are capable of being."*
>
> —Johann Wolfgang von Goethe

QUESTION NO. 3: HOW CAN I SHOW YOU I CARE?

In places that range from the dazzling Metronome Ballroom in San Francisco to the headquarters of G.E. Capital in Fairfield, Connecticut, I've asked thriving leaders, "How do you show employees you care?" By far the most frequent answer is: Show them appreciation. And in fact, the most exhilarated leaders I know are predisposed to express heartfelt gratitude for something that's real. Nothing has impact like an immediate and direct statement of appreciation. Some of my favorite examples are shown in the sidebar.

SHOWING YOUR APPRECIATION

- Call in an employee just to say thank you; don't discuss any other issue.

- Ask *your* boss to express appreciation to one of your employees.

- Leave a handwritten note to say thank you. In this age of emails and impersonal distribution lists, a handwritten note of appreciation is special.

No employee remembers a bonus from five years ago, but many remember kind words delivered by a leader about a job well done.

I recently attended a luncheon at the home of a client, Deborah, one of the few female members of the executive team of an investment firm. The beneficiary of countless promotions and accolades, Deborah boasts a salary package of well over $500,000 a year. That made it even more surprising when I stumbled across an aged but elegantly framed note card hanging proudly in her den. It read:

> *Dear Deborah,*
>
> *I'm hearing great things about your efforts. I want you to know how much I value your creativity, attention to detail and hunger for learning. Keep using these strengths and they will serve you well. Thanks for your dedication.*
> *Best,*
>
> *Walter Charles, Vice President*
> *September 22, 1982*

Surely Mr. Charles has long forgotten the minute or two when he scribbled out these words of gratitude. But his appreciation had an inspiring impact. He could not have known that more than twenty years later it would still serve as a treasured memento from a caring leader to a fledgling supervisor—and through the years, a reminder to Deborah to do the same for others.

I'd like to share a recent experience to show that Deborah's story is representative of many. The Breakfast Club is a group of advisers who give feedback on my writing projects. Each of the club's five members has at least twenty years of leadership experience. At a meeting reviewing early drafts of this chapter all five admitted that they've kept every memento of appreciation they received from various bosses through the years. This offers yet another testament to the power of a simple statement of appreciation.

"The deepest principle in human nature is the craving to be appreciated."

—William James

THE GOOD, THE BAD, AND THE UGLY

Alex, the Cleveland office manager of a pharmaceutical company, was grateful for the efforts of his staff. Their annual sales conference, attended by all the big shots from corporate headquarters, had been wildly successful. The morning after the event each employee was given a shiny gold box with a single chocolate truffle inside. The gesture was an effective act of thanks and a rather obvious one at that. What makes Alex so special though, is that he uses appreciation all the time, even when things are falling apart.

For example, not long ago Alex and his people made a major sales pitch. In spite of a week's worth of arduous preparation their client was unimpressed. And the harder the team tried, the less enthusiastic the client became. When the disaster was over, Alex called everyone together. "Before we analyze what happened," he said, "let me tell you how grateful I am for your professionalism and tenacity. I was watching all of you in there. I felt proud of your dedication and valiant attempts to make it work."

Even though Alex's boss was upset by what happened, Alex's appreciation of his people's performance during the presentation lifted their spirits and diffused his own stress. That's the personal payoff for appreciation.

And appreciation has an additional payoff. As leaders, we're enveloped in a whirlwind of events just passed and new ones impending. It's easy to fixate on the meeting that didn't go well yesterday or worry about what might come tomorrow. That fleeting moment between "just passed" and "about to happen" is hard to grasp. By focusing on what there is to appreciate now, even when things aren't going well, you stand the best chance to be engaged in the moment. And being rooted in the moment is the most productive place for a leader to be.

THE ULTIMATE TESTAMENT TO RULE 6

I looked forward to my interview with Tim, a manager who mystified me. Tim was known for seamlessly achieving great results year after year. I'd met him only briefly at several company retreats, pegging him as a tough, no nonsense kind of guy—anything but the stereotypical version of the kindly, warm, appreciative people person. As a result, I couldn't quite grasp what accounted for the crackling energy of his high-morale team. When we finally got the chance to sit down face to face I asked how he keeps his staff so productive and himself free from the clutches of LeaderShock. I fully expected him to credit his success to a solid business strategy but what he said gave me a new appreciation for the power of Rule 6. His reply: "I pay attention to my staff before anything else." How? For one thing, he conducts nontraditional manager meetings with his three supervisors every two weeks. "We don't launch into a review of numbers or clients; we make it a people review. We study each employee's performance, the successes and struggles—both professional and personal—and then map out what we need to do to make things better.

"I look at it logically." Tim said. "My employees' problems are my problems. I have a choice. I can either ignore their needs or help address them." That's why Tim can give you a rundown on every one of the forty-two people in his department. Here's a bottom-line, results-based leader who knows what priorities his employees are managing, their hobbies, and the names of every one of their kids. And they know about him, too. This non-touchy-feely leader's best business strategy is to have a genuine interest and personal relationship with each of those under his command. Why is it his best strategy? The number one reason people stay in jobs today is the quality of their relationship with their manager. Year after year the data is the same. What pushes people to quit is not their compensation or even the nature of the work but a poor relationship with their boss.

"A leader is someone who helps improve the lives of other people or improve the system they live under."

—Sam Houston

Focusing on your people first is imperative, but focusing on yourself is equally important. And how do you take care of yourself in the era of Leader-Shock? The surprising answer lies in Rule 7.

SUMMARY OF RULE SIX

LeaderShock Trap No. 6:
The Customer Addict

To please customers, we give them first priority at the expense of giving time and attention to our employees. Without taking care of our employees first, we're actually not taking care of the customers.

New Intentions

- I never take my attention off my people and their problems, both professional and personal. I understand each person has only so much to give, so when I help eliminate people's problems, they have more to contribute.

- I show my people they come first by finding out the answers to three essential questions.

  - What do you need?
  - What motivates you?
  - How can I show you I care?

- I translate the answers into concrete objectives for the way I work with them every day.

7

GIVE,
DON'T TAKE!

*"By always taking out and never putting in,
the bottom is soon reached."*

—Spanish proverb

'Tis better to give than to receive. Everyone supports the theory, but few put it to work when times turn turbulent. Under the sway of LeaderShock, managers tend to take, rather than give. And at first glance there appears to be logic to their strategy. When time, people, and money are scarce, who can afford to help others? Accumulation becomes the objective. These leaders are pushed by their cultures to *get* results, *gain* resources, *gather* information, *keep* control, and *protect* their business units.

What they don't see is that when you take, take, take, eventually the well runs dry. Slowly but surely this *survival* mentality isolates you from a community that could be your support system. You're caught in the "every man for himself" trap of LeaderShock—all because you fail to acknowledge the power of giving.

Thriving leaders have made an active shift from a *survival* mentality to one of *prosperity*. The philosophy behind this shift is eloquently illustrated by a simple Chinese proverb: "If you always give, you will always have." How does that apply to leadership? Put simply, *thriving leaders know that you get what you want by giving other people what they want.* It works like an investment with increasing dividends, water pouring back into the well.

So if you want people to support your initiatives, first support them in theirs. If you want ongoing feedback, give ongoing feedback to others. If you want to use another department's resources, first offer them some of yours. It's what I call the Marketplace of Giving, and it makes a leader's life infinitely easier.

THE MARKETPLACE OF GIVING

In the Marketplace of Giving, when somebody needs something, somebody provides it and the system pays off profitably for everyone. The giving and receiving become a cycle. As a leader you can activate the Marketplace of Giving with anyone, at any time, by offering up the best of what you have to give—skills, materials, resources, knowledge, experience, emotional support, and even the sweat and toil of your own labor. Having initiated the Marketplace, when you need something, there's a great likelihood you'll get it from someone in your marketplace.

This is not dissimilar to the efficient model of the age-old barter economy. In the small towns of the past, one neighbor crocheted shawls for the community, another made candles, a third preserved fruit, a fourth cut wood, and so on. In such a generous community with an active Marketplace of Giving, everyone is warmly dressed, has gentle candlelight, enjoys fruit through the winter and has wood for the fire. Conversely, in a town of resource hoarders, one person might have twenty shawls but no fruit, light, or warmth. It's clear in which community any one individual will thrive.

THE LEADER WHO HAS EVERYTHING

Susan, an advertising manager, has created a workplace community in which she thrives by sharing the best of herself with everyone—from the receptionist to the head of the company. As swamped as she is by the frenzied pace of the advertising world, Susan is forever initiating a Marketplace of Giving with employees, clients, and colleagues.

"My Intention is to give something *every* time I meet with someone, whether it is a compliment, information, or a new lead." says Susan. As hard as it is to believe her statement, it's true. As her consultant, I speak from first-hand experience. From the first time Susan and I met she has graciously volunteered to give feedback on my manuscripts, pass on referrals for research interviews, or send along helpful articles—all with no other motive than to encourage a Marketplace of Giving between us. Her generosity has elicited my most giving self. I'm drawn to provide Susan with the best I have to offer in return.

Herein lies her grand payoff for the time she invests in giving: When Susan needs something, her wish is everyone else's command. Driven by a desire to reciprocate, people rally around Susan, protecting her from LeaderShock. Her self-created Marketplace of Giving has become a bustling bazaar of prosperity. She gives a lot, and she gets a lot. It's a big reason she's one of the happiest and most stress-free people in the office.

THE LEADER WHO HAS NOTHING

Consider the alternative: Leaders who aren't active members of the Marketplace of Giving clog the system and stagnate. I've watched Jody, a bright, hard-working education manager with the forward momentum of a high-speed train, descend deeper and deeper into LeaderShock. And here's why: Because she's desperately trying to keep her head above water, she thinks solely in terms of who can supply her with what she wants. Her demands of "Can you get me this?" or "I need to borrow that" are infamous among her peers. Because they know she'll give nothing back, most people don't respond and Jody's train is derailed. Jody can't see that she sabotages herself by manipulating others to get resources. With this lack of generosity, she sets herself outside the system and eventually loses out. Why? Because networks of people are always more powerful than any one person.

"He who obtains has little. He who scatters has much."

—Lao Tzu

THE TRUST NETWORK

The most highly evolved form of the Marketplace of Giving is a phenomenon called simply the "Trust Network." Trust Networks are made up of groups of people who feel safe enough to say anything to one another and find mutual support in the trials and tribulations of leadership. Why are they so special? The principal purpose of these groups is the exchange of candid feedback. Sometimes informal in nature, sometimes formal, Trust Networks constitute a clear-cut mark of distinction between thriving leaders and struggling managers. Plainly put, thriving leaders have Trust Networks, Leader-Shocked managers don't.

The only way to create a high-level Trust Network is to find a handful of reliable individuals in your organization whose Intention to help you is as strong as your Intention to help them. Once you do, carve out some ground rules. The sidebar provides an example of the guiding principles set by one successful network.

GROUND RULES FOR A TRUST NETWORK

- We say anything—no matter how risky, wacky, or politically incorrect—without fear of reprisal.

- We bounce ideas off one another to address current issues.

- We exchange caring but uncensored feedback.

- We provide support and encouragement for new, risky challenges and undertakings.

- We never break confidentiality.

Gradually, your Trust Network should take on the characteristics of any other healthy ecosystem— a rainforest, a trout stream, or a beehive. All the parts function individually yet help sustain one another.

That's why Trust Networks naturally encourage each participant to be the best he or she can be.

I've actually seen splendid examples of these networks at work all over the world. I'd like to share two of them.

CEO OF HIS OWN PERSONAL ADVISORY BOARD

Gilles, a middle manager in Paris, has a Trust Network composed of four diverse one-on-one advisory relationships he relies on for guidance on a wide range of issues. He and the group of advisers agreed that they would make themselves available to Gilles, and he would be available to them, at the drop of a hat. He picks and chooses the person to tap for help based on the nature of his problem. However, when faced with a particularly troubling or complex issue, Gilles assembles all four members for what he calls an emergency Personal Advisory Board Meeting. What ensues is a crackling, no holds barred session of probing questions, advice, and encouragement. "Knowing my Board is there to guide me with career decisions, talk to me about a difficult people problem, or just support me when I really feel stuck, gives me the confidence to tackle all the obstacles I couldn't master alone." Why are his Board members so loyal? Gilles has also helped each of them through their own leadership difficulties.

A HIGH-TECH CONNECT

When you're in a crisis, Trust Networks can mean the difference between a severe case of LeaderShock and realizing your dreams. Back in 1999 during a revenue slump, a group of five managers at a midsized Silicon Valley company took the bull by the horns. Instead of closing ranks, this group opened them. Without funds for formal leadership training and in need of support, they created their own learning network dubbed the Leadership Forum. Once a week they'd convene during lunch to dissect the latest leadership books, share their trials and tribulations, and kick around new approaches to leadership issues.

As the company's fortunes declined, the other thirty or so managers became increasingly distracted by worries about their uncertain futures. The Leadership Forum, on the other hand, continued to meet, sharing ideas and employment leads and even helping each other construct resumes. When the company finally closed its doors a year later, all five were coping significantly better than the other managers—they were less stressed, more optimistic, and felt more connected to one another. Even after the company folded, this cohesive group still gathered once a week. In a poetic end to the story, three of the members went on to live their dreams—they created their own company and have recently found investors to fund its launch.

The Marketplace of Giving is also a salve to those on-the-job irritants that contribute to our sense of LeaderShock—our workplace adversaries.

DISARMING YOUR ADVERSARY

Your Marketplace of Giving is the route to transforming your most adversarial relationships from competitive to cooperative. In Rule 6, I pointed out that all people want to be respected and to feel worthwhile. So by following the give-first rule, if you want respect from your antagonists, your best means of getting it is to show respect first. That's what Yuki did after a particularly contentious conversation with Bill, the curmudgeonly I.T. programmer assigned to her department. They were unable to agree on what Yuki needed and what Bill was prepared to deliver so Bill's tone turned mean spirited and climaxed with a rather sour "You people just don't understand."

Yuki made an unannounced visit to Bill's desk the following morning. And, she came bearing gifts. Gifts come in many forms. Yuki brought the gifts of respect and understanding. She said, "Bill, I've had a chance to sit back and put myself in your shoes. I understand that this is a more complicated request than I knew. What would happen if I helped make things easier for you? If you're agreeable, I'd like you to educate me as to where I can simplify my request so that I can go back to the drawing board and present you with something that's doable." Her giving disarmed Bill because he's used to being greeted with the same attacking tone that he puts out. Yuki's urge to respect first and then find a win-win opportunity was a masterful combination. Bill became not only her ally but a true supporter. In the end, Yuki got what she needed from Bill *and* had the satisfaction of knowing how competently she handled the situation.

"Let me embrace thee, sour adversity, for wise men say it's the wisest course."

—William Shakespeare,
Henry VI

THE MARKETPLACE TO THE RESCUE

I'd like to conclude this chapter with the ultimate affirmation of Rule 6. This story features a friend and fellow business consultant, Ron, who spent a lifetime creating and collecting wonderful training materials, program ideas, and experiential exercises.

He built a career presenting seminars based on this library of materials. To his credit, he always shared this library freely, giving away copies of his materials to other consultants, even though they were his direct competition in a highly competitive field. Ron didn't see them as enemies, though. He saw them as part of his community—comrades who understood the world of the independent consultant. His giving included those trying to break into the field even though they had nothing to give in return. These people became a professional family and were happy to be at the receiving end of Ron's generosity.

One day a fire gutted Ron's office. Nothing but ashes remained of his computer and cabinets full of files. Thirty years' worth of irreplaceable work was lost. Or so he thought. When colleagues learned of his loss, everyone stepped up to help. They supported him as he had once supported them by providing copies of everything he had so unselfishly given to them—along with additional material from their own collections. Within a few weeks, Ron's library was larger than ever.

Ron's story illustrates the obvious advantage of seeing others as allies rather than as competition. One of the joys of leadership is passing on your knowledge *without fear* that the recipients will look better than you, get more business than you, or receive more recognition. So even if you are part of a competitive corporate environment, remember Ron and know that your leadership is enhanced by the degree to which you are willing to give. The Marketplace you create will come back to provide for you when you most need it.

Giving is itself the greatest gift, and as you'll learn in the next chapter, the single best gift is truth.

> *"It is one of the most beautiful compensations of this life that no man can sincerely try to help another without helping himself."*
>
> —Ralph Waldo Emerson

SUMMARY OF RULE SEVEN

Leadership Trap No. 7: The Shortsighted Taker

When we find ourselves merely trying to survive the pressures created by limited time, money, and people resources, we tend to take as much as we can. This survival mentality eventually isolates us from a community that could otherwise provide us with everything we want.

New Intentions

- I activate a Marketplace of Giving by freely sharing my knowledge, skills, materials, resources, experience, emotional support, and physical labor with as many colleagues as possible. I understand that the best way to get what I want is to give others what they want.

- I build a Trust Network with people in my organization whose Intentions to support me are as strong as my Intentions to support them. I rely on the network to guide me through the toughest times rather than isolating myself.

- I turn around poor relationships by giving rather than competing.

8

DEMAND
THE TRUTH

"People ask the difference between a leader and a boss. . . . The leader works in the open and the boss in covert."

—Theodore Roosevelt

I've watched leaders on three continents suffer needlessly as they tried to sidestep embarrassment, conflict; and hurting others' feelings by avoiding the truth. Instead, they embrace a subtle, discreet, and withholding posture that sometimes parades as politeness, in an attempt to protect themselves and others. Unfortunately, their efforts only backfire and they end up with a loss of credibility, cynical employees, and a colossal case of LeaderShock. The trap in Rule No. 8 is the Well-Meaning Withholder, a vestige of a more naïve era in management history, held over at great expense. We must usher in a new era.

What era is it? *It's the era of leaders who tell the truth, and who are willing to hear the truth!* Without truth we cannot do anything wise. It's the social contract that binds human beings together and it's a leader's means of inspiring and inviting reflection.

"Truth has no special time of its own. Its hour is now."

—Albert Schweitzer

Truth, or the lack thereof, is more publicly discussed now than in any other time in history. What we know is that the absence of truth destroys careers and organizations and has an incalculable social cost. Truthfulness, on the other hand, keeps politicians, small business owners, corporate executives, and leaders of all varieties out of the worst scourges of LeaderShock as it enhances the public good.

So let's reexamine a debilitating assumption: We tend to fear that people will pull away if we're honest. But if delivered properly, the wisdom inherent in accountable, nonattacking truth, draws people to you like a magnet. Even if the news is bad, people want to know what's real and they rally around truth tellers.

Thriving leaders know that without a steady diet of truth they can't feel secure with their team members, can't rely on information, and can't know whether their decisions are based on good business practices. They understand that in addition to building a culture of accountability, they must also build a *culture of feedback*—an environment where everyone's honest thoughts and perceptions are freely shared. Why is this so critical? For one reason, having a culture of feedback is the best way to build trust. And trust is the number one characteristic of any successful group, be it a football team, a corporation, or a government.

This chapter shows you how to take the honesty you used in stating your Intentions and invest it in the daily feedback you give to your team. You'll also see how to elicit feedback from your team as well. The challenge is in how to create an environment that makes people feel more comfortable engaging in unbridled honesty than they feel without it. Read on, as we untangle the trap of the Well-Meaning Withholder and tap into the extraordinary power of a truth-telling culture. We'll start with potent ways to *get* the truth.

> *"In order that all men may be taught to speak the truth, it is necessary that all should learn to hear it."*
>
> —Samuel Johnson

THE COURAGE TO HEAR THE TRUTH

In many environments, just hearing the word "feedback" is enough to send people into a state of panic. Some would rather face a firing squad than be subjected to a verbal critique. So let's inject a little truth right here: When we see feedback as negative, or give all our power to the person giving the feedback, we set ourselves up for a long, hard fall. I've watched competent leaders receive well meaning feedback and walk away feeling worthless and defeated, unable to sleep for days, and in some cases even plotting revenge against the person who gave the feedback. All this angst is a direct result of the way they choose to view that feedback.

THE NEW INTENTION

The first step toward a culture of feedback is a dramatic repositioning of your thinking. Your new Intention is: *To see feedback as nothing more than new information; never as an attack.* When you're committed to this mindset, critique becomes unthreatening and *useful* data. You come to realize that feedback simply reveals a fact or perception that already exists in at least one person's mind. The difference is, now you have the considerable advantage of knowing about it. You've been given the power to make better, more realistic choices.

Let's turn to the concepts that define truth telling and the techniques that make it possible. To help position your thinking, I invite you to embrace the 1 percent factor.

THE 1 PERCENT FACTOR

The 1 percent factor is based on the notion that at least 1 percent of any feedback is true. It pushes you to ask yourself, "What part of this feedback might be useful to me?" Maybe it's only 1 percent. Perhaps it's 10 percent, or even 50 percent. Maybe it all rings true. In this way, the 1 percent factor helps you avoid the worthless urge to focus on all the reasons the feedback isn't valid. It moves you away from defending yourself and toward things you can do something about.

I'd like to tell the story of one leader who took the first step in initiating a culture of feedback by putting herself out on the front line.

HEARING THE WHOLE TRUTH

Julie, the head of a government services agency, is a self-driven, fast-moving, intelligent person. When I first met her she was also a beleaguered leader, frustrated beyond belief with the twelve account representatives she inherited the year before. Julie described them as a team without trust. They couldn't be sure of one another's motives, and their hyperdiscreet environment was pervaded by dishonesty. Though I could tell Julie wasn't a participant in the backbiting I'd heard about, I challenged her to look at her part in creating the climate in which such problems thrived. Specifically, I encouraged her to use two tools for clearing the way to hear the whole truth: (1) see feedback as new and valuable information, and (2) employ the 1 percent factor. Here's what happened.

The day after Julie and I talked, we held a meeting with her team. Boldly standing before the group, she set the stage for truthfulness, "My Intention is to really hear what you have to say about my leadership." she began. "I ask that you be brutally honest with me just as I'll pledge my honesty to you. I want to do things differently and I need your help to figure out what. Anything you share with me will be a gift." At this point, Julie followed my counsel and began with the most truthful statement she could make to the group (at that moment). "I have to admit, I feel a little vulnerable up here," she confessed.

Julie began with the first of her two questions: "I want to know specific things about my leadership that are working well." They found much to compliment. She was seen as high on integrity, true to her word, and a great champion of the department. Julie recorded all this on a flipchart for everyone to see.

Having established a precedent for telling the truth, Julie jumped into what they'd all been dreading. Putting a new heading on the flipchart, she turned to face the group, "Now I'd like you to apply that same level of honesty as you tell me things about my leadership that *aren't* working." They were slow to start, but with Julie's continuous encouragement of their candor, the group's list grew and grew.

The real success of the meeting resulted from how Julie responded to that list. Had she simply told the group, "Thanks, I'll try to work on these things."

and sat down, she'd have elicited skepticism and lost all the momentum the group built. Instead, Julie systematically addressed the comments with uncensored honesty, telling them what she was, and wasn't, willing to do about each issue. In every case, she gave her reasons. Some of those issues and her responses appear in the sidebar "Julie's Handling of Employee Feedback."

JULIE'S HANDLING OF EMPLOYEE FEEDBACK

Group's Feedback: "You need to initiate stronger, friendlier relationships with us—the members of your department. Come around and talk to us more."

Julie's Response: "I know I need to devote more time to each of you, and I'm willing to commit to doing that. One thing you may not know about me is that I'm actually very shy, so I think I'm going to need your help to meet this request."

(Julie's simple admission of shyness came as a surprise to her team. Because they respected her strong will and professional competence, they'd assumed the reason she had so little personal contact was that she didn't care. This new insight for the group sent Julie's personal stock soaring because of her willingness to be vulnerable in such a guarded environment.)

Group Feedback: "Shift your priorities and put the succession planning project at the top of your list. We need it."

Julie's Response: "This is something I don't want to change because the company is about to reorganize, and it doesn't make sense to analyze staffing patterns until we know what's going to happen. As you know the performance appraisal project is my top priority, and I'm not willing to change that now."

(While some group members were taken aback by Julie's answer, at least they now understood that succession planning would not be a lead initiative and why. This illustrates a key point: Honesty generates trust, and trust comes from openness in not agreeing with people or catering to them.)

Group Feedback: "Spend less time working with the company's executive group and more time interfacing with our internal customers."

Julie's Response: "My boss has communicated that influencing the executive team is a big part of my job, and frankly, that's the only reason this department has had so much companywide impact. On the other hand, I sense that there are issues with our customers that require my support. I'd like to hear what they are so I can help you address them in a different way."

(Julie's willingness to be open and nondefensive gave her the pulse of her team and gave the team new understandings. They now knew her pressures from above, how she saw her role, and that her focus on executives was not because of an indifference to their customers.)

There are many ways to request feedback from your people but Julie's approach is among my favorites for its simplicity and power in getting issues out on the table. If you try this approach, be aware that you might find yourself in worse shape than when you started unless you carefully follow several rules:

- Use Intentions and rewards: Ramp up to the honesty with an authentic Intention statement, which sets the stage. Be sure to reward people as they contribute feedback. Remember, it's candor you want to reward, not the specific content of one piece of feedback versus another.

- If you ask for honesty, when you get it, embrace it. The slightest bit of defensiveness on your part and it's all over. If your people withhold their feedback, analyze why it might not be safe for them to speak, and do your part to change that.

- Never promise anything you're not committed to doing. The proof is in the pudding. In the weeks following our meeting, Julie's staff saw her making efforts to meet their needs and keep her promises. Their allegiance grew and grew, and so did their level of trust.

Julie's example shows how to encourage and respond to feedback from your team. This is an essential ingredient in the LeaderShock prescription, but taken by itself, it's incomplete. Beyond eliciting the truth from others, your next objective is having the courage to deliver the truth.

"Honesty is the first chapter in the book of wisdom."

—Thomas Jefferson

THE COURAGE TO TELL THE TRUTH

Thriving leaders don't shy away from giving needed feedback. They find their courage in an approach that's *tough but caring*—hard on the issue but with ultimate respect for the person. When you follow their approach, *your sole Intention in giving feedback is to be helpful and honest, never to hurt or damage anyone.* Your reason for giving the feedback has to be pure. Scrutinize your motives. Feedback given to satisfy a malicious intent destroys everyone. When you stick to this mantra, "I help, not hurt," you can't go wrong. Even if the other person doesn't like what you have to say, you know you've told the truth accountably. That's your job as a leader.

Like so many other practices in this book, the *tough but caring* approach *always* begins with an Intention statement explaining your own thoughts and motivations for giving the feedback. This has been the missing ingredient in sloppy, misinterpreted coaching and feedback sessions. Once employees know where you're coming from, then, and only then, you are positioned to lay out the issue. Make sure to allow plenty of time for employee reactions, look for opportunities to brainstorm ways to address the issue, and always close with appreciation and support.

I saw the LeaderShock consequences of dodging the truth when I worked with a popular nonprofit organization well known for the good cause they support. Regrettably, there's a disconnect between their benevolent reputation and what goes on behind closed doors. To put it bluntly, the full-time staff hate one another. It all boils down to one factor. Jim, the leader, doesn't tell the truth. Jim's got one truth for person A and another for person B. He'll tell everyone what he thinks they want to hear, and therein lies the conflict. Everyone on the team is a good person, but the infighting is out of control and it's having a devastating effect on fundraising. Lack of cooperation has caused fundraising campaigns to perform poorly, donations have fallen off, and the organization has had to cut back on the services it provides. Here's the irony: Jim's reason for not being more forthright is, "I'm afraid to disappoint anyone. These people are emotionally volatile. If I upset them too much, they'll quit." Jim's dishonesty exacerbates the toxic emotions and unwittingly creates an unproductive and hurtful environment. The health of the organization is compromised as a result of a fearful leader. If Jim wants a turnaround in results, his most critical role is not only to hold his people accountable for their behavior, but also to be courageous enough to tell it like it is.

> *"A real leader faces the music, even when he doesn't like the tune."*
>
> —Anonymous

THERE'S AN ELEPHANT IN THE ROOM

Not too long ago I was working with Darnell, the division head of a training and development company, and his five lieutenants. My charge for the day was to assist the group in uncovering impediments to their financial success. Something indefinable wasn't right. When I arrived they proudly presented me with a list of items they supposed likely to increase revenue. I could tell that their list didn't get to the heart of the real problems. It included such generic items as: *Develop new leads in two territories. Redefine roles to focus on new business. Enhance communication on this team.*

"Let me challenge you." I said. "My guess is these aren't really the underlying issues. Something tells me there are some elephants in this room." "Elephants" are those organizational beasts that everyone sees but no one talks about. But, they are undeniable truths. In our personal lives they might be unspeakable family issues like Uncle Charlie's drinking or Mom's gambling. For business leaders, the symbolic elephant is something everyone worries about but doesn't dare mention, at least publicly. Regardless of cause, the elephant runs rampant through the office with its unspoken power and prevents us from realizing the results we desire. If it's allowed to remain unleashed, the elephant grows until it fills the entire office, suffocating its victims. I've seen it crush leaders and entire companies.

On this day, I could almost smell the group's fear. My intuition told me there was more than one elephant in the room, so I challenged them to an elephant hunt. You could have heard a pin drop. I let the silence hang, until finally Darnell, the leader, broke the ice. "The truth is that we don't want to admit that although this team believes it's headed in the right direction, everyone else in the company thinks it isn't. I think we need to talk about that." Heads around the room nodded. Eyes began to make contact. Team members began chiming in. They'd all secretly worried about that same thing.

Darnell's words opened a door everyone could walk through, and the team took its cue from him. By the time we finished our hunt, eleven elephants had been corralled. Now deeper, scarier, underlying issues were on the table, and the team could talk openly and productively about how to respond. Some of what they said included:

- We don't have a culture of accountability. If our managers (and staff) don't support company initiatives, we let them off the hook.

- Our margins are under pressure because we're marketing a Mercedes product to a Chevrolet audience that wants only the basics.

- Next year, after Jonathan Black retires, we'll have no supporter on the executive board.

- One member of this team, Sharon, seems apathetic and checked-out.

By naming the elephants in the room lots of good unfolded at the meeting:

- Sharon revealed the source of her apathy.

- The real obstacles were dealt with.

- Leaders got a chance to unload stress.

- The group bonded around honesty.

- Secondary business issues were dealt with more effectively because the primary issues were cleared away.

- The precedent set here made the team's approach to other issues more honest and forthright.

Like Darnell, you can do much the same with your team. Before your next departmental meeting, ask team members to write down their top three elephants, or work-related stresses. An anonymous solicitation sometimes works best. Transcribe the results on a flipchart and share it as part of the meeting. Then engage the group, zeroing in on the real elephants, corralling them, and getting them out of the group's way.

The escalation of LeaderShock is directly proportional to the number of issues left unacknowledged and unexpressed. As uncomfortable as it is to name those unacknowledged issues, if you don't do so, you doom your team to working on a never-ending stream of their effects.

> *"Our lives begin to end the day we become silent about things that matter."*
>
> —Martin Luther King

MY TRUTH

Now that you've got some tools for getting and giving feedback, we need to discuss the truth about truth. We don't all see things in the same way. A group of twenty employees can witness the same event and come away with twenty different truths about (or versions of) what happened. This points up the importance of a concept called "my truth." "My truth" can best be understood by imagining that each of us is a camera, fitted with a unique lens. Each lens yields a perspective all its own. Our lenses are affected by our cultural background, life experience, and genetics. They are also mediated by our emotional framework and the degree to which we are invested in the event we're viewing. So although we are all looking at the same scene, our image of that scene, our truth, is anywhere from a little different to vastly different from others' images. The snapshot we take away preserves these differences and becomes our picture of reality.

With so many different truths, how do leaders get everyone to agree? They don't. That's why thriving leaders have given up the idea of finding group consensus. This remnant of a 1990s leadership ideology remains with us today only as a symptom of LeaderShock. We waste time trying to agree on what's true and what isn't—as though there were just one absolute truth. Those differences all contribute to a rich, more complete understanding of the issues at hand. As a leader, it's your job not so much to select from among them, but to help integrate them into a comprehensive perspective as the basis for good decisions. It's neither effective nor efficient to figure out who's right and who's wrong because most of the time everyone has a legitimate perspective. The best we can do, particularly in the age of LeaderShock, is to take everyone's perspective into account, then use the diversity of information it yields to make well-informed decisions. There's no guarantee we'll always be victorious, but we certainly have a much better shot at it.

"You cannot change the truth, but the truth can change you."

—Anonymous

Leaders get swallowed up by the effects of LeaderShock when they give in to a fear of honesty. Honoring people with the truth and being willing to hear it sets everyone free. When we incorporate truth along with the other seven rules presented in this book, the effect is remarkable. We can rise above management chaos to celebrate the rewards that come from real leadership.

SUMMARY OF RULE EIGHT

LeaderShock Trap No. 8:
The Well-Meaning Withholder

When we protect ourselves from embarrassment, conflict, or hurt feelings by withholding truthful feedback or avoiding hearing the truth from the people around us, we're at a grave disadvantage. We lose credibility and the knowledge critical to our success.

New Intentions

- I tell the truth to everyone around me by embracing a tough but caring approach— hard on the issue but with ultimate respect for the person. I always begin any feedback with an Intention statement revealing my motives.

- I emphatically search out the truth. I see feedback only as new information, and use the 1 percent rule to focus on the part of the feedback that's helpful, rather than defending myself.

- I take everyone's truth into consideration when I make decisions and then use what I hear to make the best choice.

SYNERGY

A NEW WAY
TO LEAD

You've experienced each of the eight rules individually. Now I want to bring them together as they're meant to be, integral parts of a synergistic leadership system. This system becomes your template for an extraordinary new way to lead, a behavioral roadmap to approaching every aspect of leadership. Best visualized as a circular model, when all the rules are fully operational they generate power and exhilaration.

This model is analogous to our solar system. Like the Sun, Intention is at the center. With its powerful energy, Intention's gravitational pull keeps the other seven rules in alignment. These seven rules are like the individual planets, each a viable

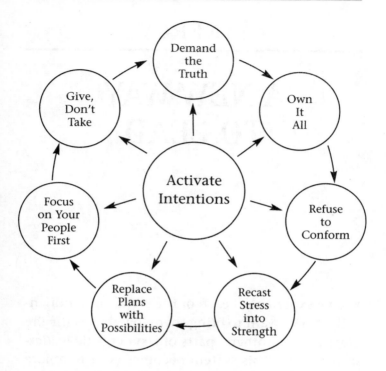

world unto itself. The whole system can't function optimally without each rule operating fully on its own while exerting force on the others to keep the system balanced.

Think of it this way: If *Giving* (Rule 7) is so beneficial why don't thriving leaders give all their time to helping other managers? They don't because that would make it impossible to implement Rule 6 — *Focus on Your People First.* Then imagine how difficult it would be to *Refuse to Conform* (Rule 3) if you adhere to traditional ways of doing your leadership job, rather than creatively *Opening Up Possibilities* (Rule 5). And if *Demanding the Truth* (Rule 8) means freely sharing your opinions and perceptions, why don't leaders feel free to blame others for things that aren't going well? The answer is twofold: first, they wouldn't be *Owning It All* (Rule 2), and second, blaming someone else for stressful situations is antithetical to *Recasting Stress into Strength* (Rule 4).

As you'll see in the final story, regardless of how difficult leadership circumstances may be, when you bring all eight rules together you create a far more positive experience than would have ever seemed possible.

A LEADERSHOCK CROSSROAD

I want to share the story of a leader named Malcolm, the Assistant Manager of an Accounting Department for a consumer products company. A year ago, after being overwhelmed by LeaderShock, Malcolm set out to reengineer his approach to leadership. After embracing the eight rules, everything changed. He began stating his real Intentions for the first time. The quality of work improved and so did the quality of the work environment. People felt directed and appreciated, but most of all Malcolm felt a renewed sense of capability and power. Taking a no-blame policy, he guided staff through a difficult series of governmental and internal audits with a "What's our part?" philosophy to every systems failure and reporting error. He was flexible and successfully Recast high staff turnover and pressure from upper management. In the process he differentiated himself as a leader with special talents for connecting with people cross-functionally. Performance in his unit went way up. Everyone noticed his remarkable turnaround. Finally, Malcolm felt like he had the leadership role wired. It seemed as though there was nothing he couldn't handle.

But as any leader knows, in the era of Leader-Shock sometimes things just aren't fair. Without warning, a work-related disappointment hit Malcolm in a very personal way.

The story began when Malcolm walked out of the Finance Director's office one late afternoon. He felt as though he'd been hit in the stomach with a sledgehammer. As Assistant Manager of the Accounting department it seemed a forgone conclusion that when the top accounting manager position opened up, Malcolm would be a shoo-in. On this unfortunate morning, in fact, the accounting manager position *was* open; yet Malcolm was told that the job had been given to Walter, a manager from the West Coast whose division had recently disbanded. "Let me be honest," said the Finance Director, "You've demonstrated over the last year that you're a terrific leader, but we had to find Walter a new job. I don't expect you to like this, but I do hope you'll understand." As he felt the first twinges of a slide into despair, Malcolm once again relied upon the eight rules.

RULE 1: ACTIVATE INTENTIONS

Walking back into his office Malcolm made a pivotal move when he zeroed in on an immediate Intention. To stop the avalanche of unproductive voices and assumptions rattling around in his brain, he assertively chose an *attitude* focused on feeling good about himself, not defeated and inadequate. Moving to *behavior*, he realized that the biggest win would be in showing others how professional he really was—competent, accountable, grounded. The days ahead might be an emotional roller coaster, and there would be many additional Intentions along the way, but for now, he had adopted the most helpful state of mind.

RULE 2: OWN IT ALL

Was Malcolm a victim of corporate politics? Perhaps. Did he intend to *feel* like a victim? No. He allowed himself about two minutes of self-pity and then stopped himself from blaming Walter, the

Finance Director, or anyone else. Clear of any *self-*blame, Malcolm headed home to enjoy his family.

RULE 3: REFUSE TO CONFORM

Once Malcolm hit his office the next morning he immediately pulled out his Personal Peaks list. Administrative minutiae, lists of data and monthly spreadsheets were certainly not at the top of the list. He reminded himself that what excited him about coming into work each morning was educating other departments about the principles of finance and mentoring employees of diverse backgrounds. Later on, this self-knowledge would pay off.

RULE 4: RECAST STRESS INTO STRENGTH

Recasting turned out to be a pivotal phase in his triumphant recovery. Just knowing he had a roadmap to move through the problem gave him a sense of security and well-being. Instead of wallowing in a morass of self-doubt and endless what-ifs, he funneled his energy into each stage of the Recasting process.

During the lunch hour he challenged himself to dive into the world of pure *emotions*. He struggled to let raw feelings surface. Rejection and anger emerged as the most prevalent but there was also embarrassment. After all, there wasn't a person in the organization who didn't know that Malcolm wanted that job and wanted it badly. Understanding only too well the way the company rumor mills operated, Malcolm dreaded the thought of the sympathetic well-wishers gushing over him, or even worse, the uncomfortable coworkers who might try to avoid him altogether. Most painful of all, he surmised, would be the busy little hornets buzzing around behind his back full of gossipy critiques and half-baked theories. At this moment, coming to terms with the reality of it all, Malcolm felt even worse than he had the night before. But putting his trust in the power of Recasting, he knew he had to focus on the feelings first.

Over the next few days Malcolm used his emotions as a springboard to understanding more about himself. He searched for new insights and *meaning*. Here are some of his conclusions:

- He'd paid too much attention to getting promoted and having a manager's title and too little to learning and exploring what he really wanted in a career.

- He'd put all his professional eggs in one basket.

- He was too preoccupied with what other people thought about him.

Malcolm pondered *opportunities*. He called upon his most trusted colleagues and invited them to an early morning breakfast where they helped him look for opportunities. The brainstorming turned out to be more than just fun; the camaraderie only further built his confidence. Here are some of their suggestions for Malcolm:

- Learn from Walter, a man who enjoyed a rich network of colleagues throughout the company.

- Ask for additional assignments outside the Accounting department.

- Take time to be with your young family. The manager's job clearly would not have afforded this luxury.

RULE 5: REPLACE PLANS WITH POSSIBILITIES

The opportunities Malcolm unveiled while Recasting were certainly new options but there was something far richer. With a technically novice manager coming on board there were possibilities galore for breaking away from the confines of overplanned procedures and hard and fast job descriptions. Malcolm realized he held more power than ever before. Now, as the only one with the knowledge and capability to reorganize department structure and work-flow, he had cause to celebrate. Here was an amazing chance to find both creative ways to use his peak talent—educating—and more effectively use the talents of the staff. He was actually beginning to feel pumped up about the chances for a more satisfying work life.

RULE 6: FOCUS ON YOUR PEOPLE FIRST

Malcolm knew that the people in the department would be leery of new management in this already turbulent year. He found just the right occasion to assemble the department and share the news about the new manager along with some self-revealing truth. His words were hopeful and upbeat, but people were still worried. In the three weeks until Walter came aboard, Malcolm stayed close to the people, checking in frequently and listening to their concerns. His close relationships with staff was his favorite part of the job.

RULE 7: GIVE, DON'T TAKE!

Critical to Malcolm's success was the decision to offer up the best of himself to Walter. Rather than pull away in anger or sabotage Walter's success, he consciously planned to share his years of experience

in the department. If ever there was a time to activate a Marketplace of Giving, this was it. Malcolm
had much to give Walter but Walter could offer even
more to Malcolm.

RULE 8: DEMAND THE TRUTH

On the day Walter arrived, the two men had a
chance to sit down for the first time. "I want to tell
you the truth." Malcolm told Walter, "I wanted the
job myself and wasn't happy with the decision. But
I'm ready to move ahead. You can rely on me for
support and straight ahead honesty."

What's happening with Malcolm now? By con-
tinuing to exhibit great leadership, share his talents,
and open up new options for jobs outside of
accounting, he ended up in his dream job. He
became the Diversity Officer for the entire company.
When you follow the wisdom of the model it
keeps you on the straight and narrow. The seductive
LeaderShock traps that push you into being a *crisis-
reactor, victim, conformist, denier, rigid thinker,
customer-addict, taker, and information withholder*
are cunningly sidestepped. You give yourself the
opportunity to soar. Like Malcolm, you walk away
a true leader.

AFTERWORD

As I end the book, I recognize that this is the beginning for you, so let me take one more opportunity to suggest that you start by invoking your greatest personal freedom—to choose your Intentions and state them freely. At the risk of overkill, I leave you with this notion: *Without Intention it's difficult to do anything well. With willful Intention anything is possible!* LeaderShock will obscure your way if you function on automatic pilot.

Think of yourself as a sculptor who begins with the grand Intention to create a beautiful work of art from a chunk of marble. As you work you relentlessly support this overall Intention with smaller ones—an intentional chisel stroke here, an intentional polish there. In much the way that the block of marble takes a form that reflects your wishes as an artist, conscious Intention fortifies your dream to be the kind of leader *you* want to be—every move purposeful. Once Intention positions you on the path, the other seven rules take over to guide you along your way.

This program is not something I'm advocating from a theoretical or academic position. I'm offering it to you with personal passion and confidence. Not only has it proven successful for my clients, it is also my exclusive guide to running my own business and leading my personal life. It informs every decision. It rescues me when I falter.

While writing this book there were days when things seemed unmanageable, sometimes impossible. As I look back I see that the eight rules were always the guiding light. When I set my Intention to be confident and prolific, I broke through blocks to creativity. When I allowed myself the freedom to veer away from set-in-stone ideas and consider other possibilities for making my points, paragraphs suddenly had clarity and crackle. When I gave back something to the gracious interviewees, we all felt supported and got what we wanted. When I capitalized on my strengths and tapped into complementary talents of editors and readers, things came together faster. And, when outside obstacles threatened success, the "What's my part?" question directed me back to the courses of action that were in my power to inaugurate. In fact every time I got stuck I used the model to identify the barrier.

The same is true for you. When leadership demands overwhelm, use the model as a diagnostic tool. Assess where you need to advance behavior. Examine each rule. Ask the questions: Am I fully activating Intentions? Am I owning it all? Am I refusing to conform? Am I Recasting? And so on. If at any point your answer is "No", that's where you should focus your attention until you're back on track.

Becoming a thriving leader is a lifelong journey. As with all journeys it will not always go as expected. But now you have your roadmap. I wish you great luck on your journey and a wonderful life, balanced with personal happiness and a fulfilling career as a powerful and exhilarated leader.

For information about the LeaderShock programs, products or keynote speeches, please contact Foster, Hicks & Associates.

email: LeaderShock@FosterHicks.com
Web site: www.LeaderShock.com
phone: 510-540-6000

ABOUT THE AUTHOR

Greg Hicks is coauthor of the best-selling *How We Choose to Be Happy* and CEO of Foster, Hicks & Associates, an internationally recognized leadership consultancy whose clients range from G.E. Capital to the U.S. Navy. A sought after keynote speaker, Hicks is on the faculty of the Health Forum and the College of Business at San Jose State University and has been featured in such magazines as *Health, Working Mother,* and *Reader's Digest.* Every year thousands of leaders around the globe—from first-time managers to seasoned executives—profit from his popular and transformational Leader-Shock programs.